A COLLECTOR'S GUIDE TO

GAMES AND PUZZLES

A COLLECTOR'S GUIDE TO

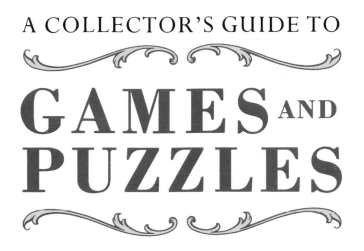

GAMES AND PUZZLES

CAROLINE GOODFELLOW

CHARTWELL
BOOKS, INC.

A QUINTET BOOK

Published by Chartwell Books
A Division of Book Sales Inc.,
110 Enterprise Avenue
Secaucus, New Jersey 07094

ISBN 1-55521-727-3

This book was designed and produced by
Quintet Publishing Limited
6 Blundell Street
London N7 9BH

Creative Director: Terry Jeavons
Designer: Stuart Walden
Project Editor: Sarah Buckley
Editor: Lydia Darbyshire
Photography: Pip Barnard

Typeset in Great Britain by
Central Southern Typesetters, Eastbourne
Manufactured in Singapore by
Chroma Graphics (Overseas) Pte. Ltd Singapore
Printed in Singapore by Kim Hup Lee Printing Co. Pte. Ltd.

ACKNOWLEDGEMENTS

I would like to express my grateful thanks to Anthony
Burton, all the staff at Bethnal Green Museum of
Childhood and Pauline Cockrill for their invaluable
assistance, to Isabel Sinden of the National Art Picture
Library of the Victoria and Albert Museum for arranging
the photographic work undertaken and especially to Pip
Barnard for his excellent photography. Grateful thanks are
also extended to Mrs. D. Boyce and Mr. S. Dance for their
permission to photograph their games.
Most appreciative thanks go to Mr. Herbert Siegel and G.
William Holland for arranging the photography, at very
short notice, of the games from the Collection of Herbert
and Jacqueline Siegel.
Three photographs were generously supplied by the Essex
Institute, Salem, Massachusetts and I would like to very
much thank Robert Weis and the Staff of the Institute for
all their co-operation.
Special thanks for all their help and encouragement are due
to Betty Ridley, Faith Eaton, Margaret and Blair Whitton,
and Josephine Goodfellow.

PHOTOGRAPHIC ACKNOWLEDGEMENTS

The majority of the games are housed at the Bethnal Green
Museum of Children, London and are reproduced by kind
permission of the Trustees of the Victoria and Albert
Museum. Photographer Pip Barnard.
Additional photographs are reproduced by the kind
permission of the Collection of Herbert and Jacqueline
Siegel (Photographer: G. William Holland), the Essex
Institute, Salem, Massachusetts, and Harry L. Rinker,
Rinker Enterprises Inc., Zionsville, Pennsylvania.

CONTENTS

INTRODUCTION

There is a magic in games that does not exist in any other form of play or toy. Games range from those created in the imagination, such as hide and seek, to simple games using a few scratchings on the ground or on paper, right through to quite sophisticated manufactured items. The equipment used for these games usually takes the form of inanimate objects, which are very often boring to look at. However, games seem to have a magnetic appeal for humans both young or old. Everyone seems to respond to the temptation to jump along a hop scotch grid sketched out roughly in chalk on a city pavement.

All games require intelligence, and many need dexterity. Some recreate the thrill of sporting activities while others give a sense of creativity. A few can even cause anger and a great deal of frustration.

However enjoyable a game may be, the one basic aim is to win, whether one is competing against oneself, against a single opponent or against several opponents. Even doing a dissected or jigsaw puzzle is a challenge. More often than not the main challenge is to keep your temper when other people come and slot in the one piece you have been looking for.

It is known from surviving records, paintings and artefacts that games very similar to those of today were played by people of the ancient civilizations centred around the Mediterranean and in the Middle and Far East. In fact, in many of the countries in these areas today, it is still possible to see people playing various board games, perhaps whiling away their spare time, discussing business or just gossiping.

Apart from jigsaw puzzles, there are only a few basic methods of playing games. However, over the past couple of hundred years, thousands of variations have been created. The basic methods of play come down to three types – the race game, the strategy game and the card game. Many were originally developed for adults and were later adapted for children.

The games also became a part of the industrial and social life of entire nations, reflecting changing ideas and ideals, particularly during periods of major upheaval.

Throughout the 18th century and well into the 19th century, the size of the middle income group of merchants, solicitors, doctors and industrialists grew ever greater. Trade flourished and unknown areas were explored. The adventurers who were prepared to open shipping routes and establish trading agreements reaped rich financial rewards. This was an age of enlightenment, invention, innovation and scientific discovery.

The upbringing of children within these middle-class families also changed dramatically. Education became essential, covering not only the 'three Rs', but sensible grounding in national and international affairs. National pride and achievements were stressed, as were faults. In general, everyone seemed to be looking outwards, to try to understand new concepts. It was in the late 18th century and early 19th century that many charity schools were founded to educate both girls and boys, although much of their education was taken up in learning the skills they could use to earn a living.

Most of the board and card games were designed for children below the age of 12. It is hard to realize that

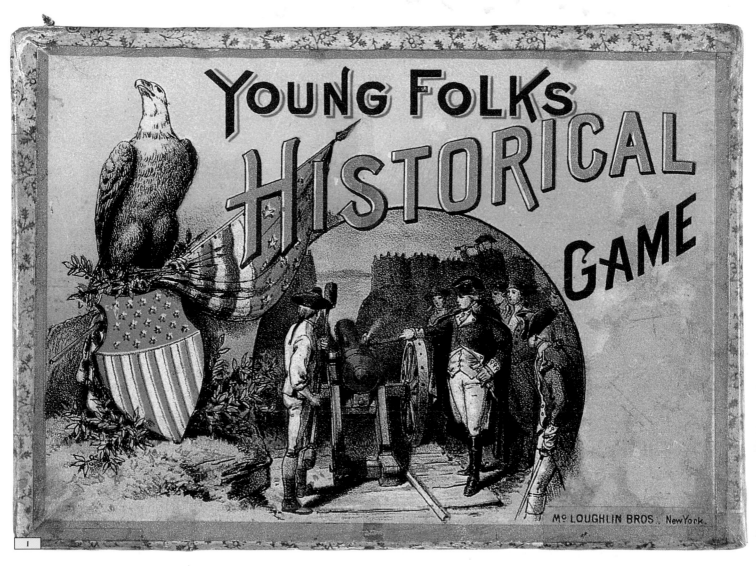

1

many of these games could not be played by children today because their vocabularies are not sufficient to cope with the texts. Nowadays we would not expect a 12-year-old to enter the family business, to become an apprentice or to enter domestic service.

The publishers of games were already established producers of maps and books, many of which were also aimed at children. The idea of producing an educational tool was, in a way, a novelty. *The Game of the Goose* was popular, and it required only a few changes to create the *Game of Human Life* or the *History of England*. The games were well received by parents who appreciated the educational aspects, the children's resulting enjoyment and possibly that the games could be played in relative peace and calm.

The early games stressed learning through play, but this aspect was gradually dropped in favour of sheer

1

In the United States at the end of the 19th century many games were still marketed for their educational content rather than as games of fun; however, the notion that learning can be fun was employed. Following closely in the footsteps of Milton Bradley's games of *Authors,* McLoughlin Brothers devised the *Young Folks Historical Game* in 1890. The 1876 Centennial celebrations renewed the country's interest in its own past and fostered the concept of American jingoism. Games and card manufacturers were eager to jump on this bandwagon in much the same way as English makers had done so. It was felt to be important in most countries to provide a national pride in a country's past.

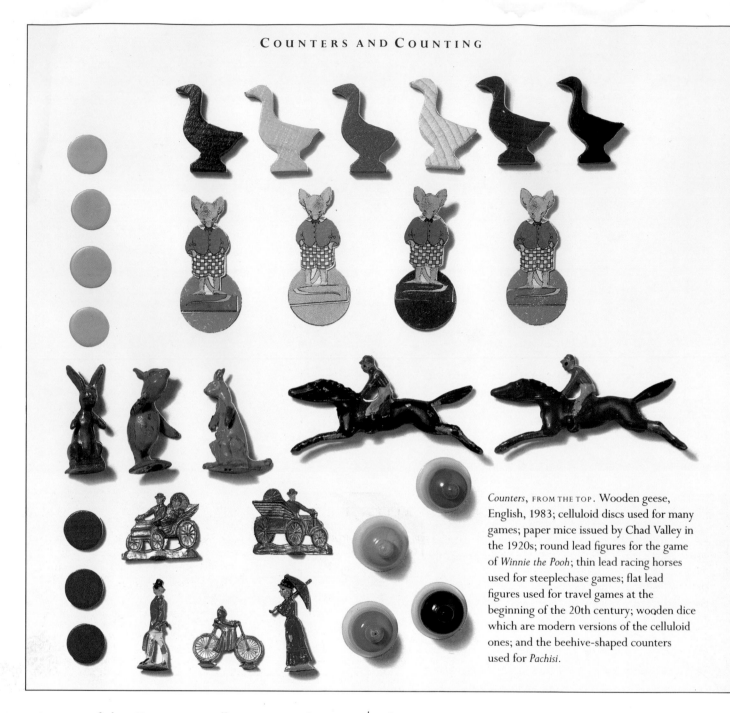

COUNTERS AND COUNTING

Counters, FROM THE TOP. Wooden geese, English, 1983; celluloid discs used for many games; paper mice issued by Chad Valley in the 1920s; round lead figures for the game of *Winnie the Pooh*; thin lead racing horses used for steeplechase games; flat lead figures used for travel games at the beginning of the 20th century; wooden dice which are modern versions of the celluloid ones; and the beehive-shaped counters used for *Pachisi*.

enjoyment of play. However, not all games were that enjoyable, regardless of the claims of their titles. More recently, games manufacturers have returned to the idea of learning through play.

Television and computers have had dramatic influences both on the subjects of the games and how they are played. Many games, lasting very short times, are merely the same game revamped with different characters. Computer games have however one major drawback – they tend to be played by one person alone, often without even contact with a parent. The solitary playing of such games can affect the learning of social skills which are needed by everyone.

Perhaps the whole logic of games as a teaching tool can be summed up in the words used by John Harris as the introduction or Advertisement to his game *Historical Pastime*, which was published in 1810:

Counting Devices, TOP LEFT CLOCKWISE. Teetotum, four-sided marked with letters, made of bone; English, early 19th century. This is a directional teetotum used for such games as *The Cottage of Content* or *Right Roads and Wrong Ways*. Another bone teetotum with six sides marked with numbers which would be used for a straightforward race game. Modern wooden dice and dice cup. 'Chausar' dice made of stone in India in the 1970s. These were used with the Indian form of *Pachisi* but could replace other forms of devices such as cowrie shells if desired. Cowrie shells could be used as either counting devices, usually by counting the open sides, or as counters.

Surprisingly few tools are actually required to play many games. Something to show a score and something to move around the playing surface is all that is needed.

JOHN WALLIS, LONDON

John Wallis, together with his sons, John Jnr and Edward, was probably the most prolific of the British publishers of games between 1775 and 1847. Wallis produced games and dissected puzzles and was followed, after his death in 1818, by Edward. During their span, a number of different addresses were recorded. The earliest address was 16 Ludgate Street, often with

the name 'Map Warehouse'; from 1805 the address was 13 Warwick Square, sometimes with the name 'Instructive Toy Warehouse'; and from 1812 to 1847, 42 Skinner Street, Snow Hill. It was this last address that was used by Edward Wallis, working either alone or in conjunction with his father as Wallis and Son or John & Edward Wallis. Most of Edward's

games show the abbreviation Edw. and occasionally one finds Ino for John. John Wallis Jnr, though often found in conjunction with his father and brother, operated independently at 188 The Strand (1806 to 1808) and as proprietor of the Marine Library, Sidmouth, Devon from 1814 to 1822. The Wallises also worked with John Harris.

The utility and tendency of this Game must be obvious at first sight; for surely there cannot be a more agreeable study than History, and none more improving to Youth, than that which conveys to them, in a pleasing and comprehensive manner, the Events which have occurred in their own Country.

The little prints, which are regularly numbered, from 1 to 158, represent either Portraits of the principal Personages who have signalised themselves

as Kings, Statesmen, Churchmen, Generals, Poets, etc., or some remarkable Occurrence in our Country. This will naturally excite a curiosity in the youthful mind; and that curiosity will be gratified in the short account of each reign subjoined. On the whole, the writer flatters himself, that the public approbation will convince him, that the hours he has devoted to the formation of this little Scheme, have not been spent in vain.

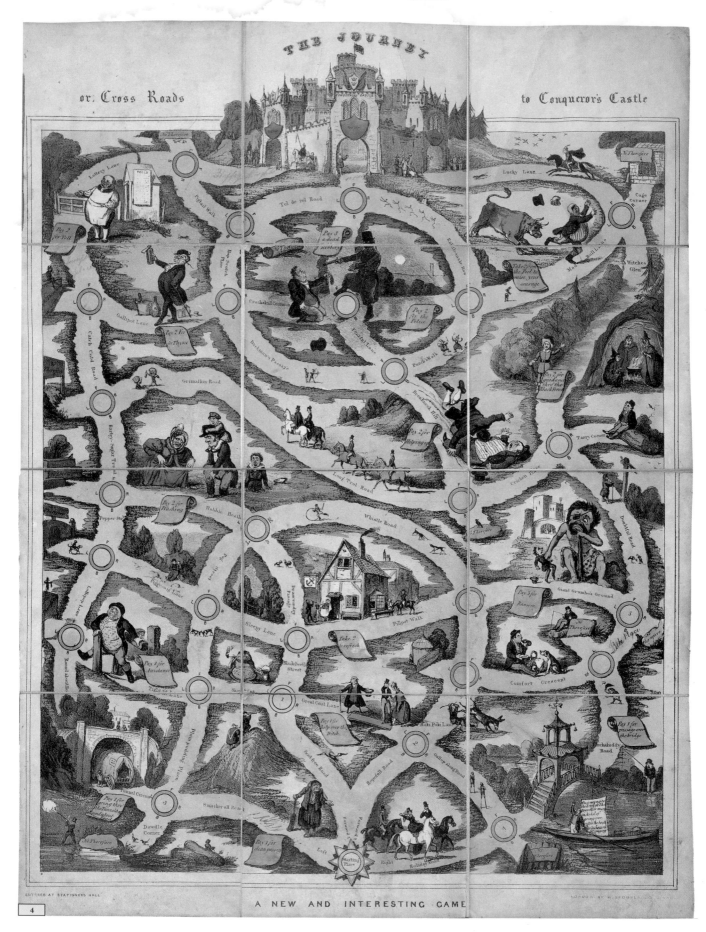

COLLECTING, CARE AND ATTENTION

Collecting games and puzzles is a hobby for everyone; these items are collected for many different reasons. The sheer thrill of playing games or constructing puzzles is a major motivation, as is the enjoyment of looking at an intriguing design or a very beautiful picture.

There are many different types of collectors too. Those who collect the items because they represent various forms of printing vie with those people collecting the work of one publisher or one type of game; in turn these collectors vie with those who enjoy games for their own sake.

As soon as a game or puzzle is dropped from production, it could be termed as collectible; however, in practice this rarely happens. Most games and puzzles produced during the last 30 or 40 years have no intrinsic value other than what a keen collector might be willing to pay. Also any such games must be in mint condition to command any price more than a few pence.

Much older games, of course, are much sought after. It is not possible to define the monetary value of any game, as any value is greatly affected by the market forces, the condition of the game itself, and the peculiarities of the buying public. What may be fashionable and expensive this year, may be more so next year, but equally its value could fall dramatically. Any

collector should decide his or her own reasons for collecting. It is usually advisable to collect items because they give the collector enjoyment. Collecting for investment may be profitable in some spheres, but when related to games and puzzles could prove to be a great disappointment.

Often the best source of supply of modern games is the jumble sale or car boot sale. Modern jigsaw puzzles may be found this way too, but another source is groups of people who enjoy doing jigsaws and will swap them.

Older games, of course, are much less likely to be found in these ways; they have become items of value and can command a great deal of money. They can be found in auction sales and with antique dealers. The problem remains the cost and a buyer must decide whether or not he or she is able to justify paying the price asked. This may be a particularly difficult decision for the person interested in the game as a game. The collector must also be aware that the games appear not in sales of toys or games but more usually in sales of printed matter, quite unrelated to games.

The collector should decide what type of game he or she would like to collect, whether it represents a game to be played or a 'work of art', and how much he or she can pay, not only for the game itself but for its preservation.

4

William Spooner was the publisher of this game, titled *The Journey* or *Cross Roads to Conqueror's Castle* (see also page 56).

When selecting a game, always check whether it is complete. Rules and equipment can be replaced or details found by following up information from other sources, including reference books. The most difficult items to replace are the booklets issued with the earlier games. Rules of play are generally obvious but the booklets contain details which the players are required to recite or answer questions upon. It is possible to make up suitable questions or details but by investigating sources such as museums it may be possible to track down a copy of a particular booklet.

Having acquired a game or puzzle, the next step is to keep it safe and intact. The earlier games, which were printed on a rag pulp paper, then mounted on a cloth sheet (usually linen), were issued with slip cases: a cardboard case into which the folded game could be placed, together with an accompanying booklet. Teetotums and counters were sometimes issued with the games, but often families already had this equipment which they used for any of the games they played. Later games came complete with all the necessary equipment to play the game. This still applies today.

Paper is greatly affected by the elements; too much light, heat or dampness can quickly result in a marked deterioration. Light (both natural and artificial) makes the paper fade and dry out. Wood pulp paper has a high acidic content, so light can cause chemical changes too. Heat, whether from radiators, hot water pipes or fires, also causes dryness; the paper may become very brittle and start to crack. Dampness causes stains and ultimately mould and can also affect the chemical balance of the paper, increasing its acidity. Fumes from fires, cooking and smoking are also potentially damaging, as are the oils emitted by one's own hands. The collector must find a balance between safeguarding the items and still being able to enjoy them.

PAPER AND PRINTING

Games have always been made from a variety of materials: stone and marble, ivory and bone, wood, and (for more than 200 years) paper. This last material, being relatively cheap to produce, lent itself to 'mass production'.

The making of paper was evolved in China and Japan; it arrived in Europe during the 12th century. Early paper had a high content of rag pulp which was replaced during the 19th century by a wood pulp mixture. This mixture, though cheaper and more abundant than rag pulp, has proved to be less stable in the long term. Nevertheless at the time it was used, it was suitable for printing on, accepting the inks and colours with ease.

Four main printing techniques were used for games, depending on the time and place of production. The majority of games published between 1770 and 1820 were engravings, either on wood or copper. The design was cut directly on to the end grain of the wood or the copper plate, resulting in a fine line drawing. The process required a craftsman with highly developed artistic and dexterity skills. The colouring of the resulting print was normally done by hand but stencils could also be used.

Another printing technique was etching, done by a number of different methods. A copper plate could be treated with acid-resistant compounds, usually beeswax and asphaltum (a hydrocarbon mixture), onto which the design would be drawn before submerging the plate into an acid bath. This was a cheaper process than engraving as the artist did not use the skills of an engraver.

Stipple engraving, often used in conjunction with other methods, marked the design with dots or small spots rather than cutting it. Its advantage was that it created shading and graduation of tones. The same applied to aquatints which used resin and nitric acid to create prints resembling ink and watercolour drawings.

Aloys Senefelder of Munich was credited with introducing lithography at the end of the 18th century. This involved printing from stone, and was based on the premise that oil and water do not mix. This method was developed into colour lithography or chromolithography towards the middle of the 19th century and is the basis for modern offset printing.

The presses began as hand-operated wooden ones, gradually being replaced by iron machines. The manpower was replaced by steam power. In fact, printers were among the first to recognize the advantages of engaging their presses to a static steam-powered engine, thus greatly reducing their workload.

All European countries published and exported games. Until the mid 19th century, the United States imported most of its games, through either wholesalers or immigrants. Many immigrants also recreated games they had played when young. Nevertheless, throughout the period distinct trends developed in each country.

In England, for example, board games were flourishing, while in Germany other paper toys were more frequently produced. Because Germany had developed lithography, which became the most common method of printing, that country's printers began to supply the rest of the world, cleverly creating toys of four languages which could be sold almost anywhere without needing modification to any of the printing processes.

When chromolithography began, designs from elsewhere were sent to Germany for printing. Some companies established their own works there, such as Spears & Sons. This company was based near London, and had their printing works near Nuremberg.

The best solution is to have a room set aside for the games, where the lighting and atmosphere is carefully controlled. Daylight should be excluded, and ultra-violet screens used on any lamps. Today cool lamps are available, but adequate measures should be taken to dissipate any heat, whether from lights or heating. As even and moderate a temperature as possible should be maintained; likewise the humidity, as too dry an atmosphere is as potentially damaging as damp conditions. The room should be as dust-proof as possible, and the casings of the games could be dust-proofed. If there is dust in the atmosphere, it quickly settles on *all* surfaces.

Circulating air is important. Games and puzzles are made from natural products which must breathe, and while polluted air is not good, some air circulation is needed.

There is always a debate about the actual handling of the items, over whether gloves should be worn or not. The argument for gloves is that they protect the paper from any oils secreted by the hands; the argument against is that the gloves impede the hands and cause physical damage; they also get dirty, thus transmitting dirt onto the paper. Perhaps handling the objects as little as possible is the solution, whether gloves are worn or not. One golden rule is never use a pen of any kind near the games.

If you decide to display some of your games, there are many archival products available – tapes, see-through plastics, acid-free paper and card. If in doubt, most museums and many libraries will be able to assist with information. Do not leave any one item on display for too long; all need a rest and by changing the display, you the owner are able to enjoy your collection.

Games have one advantage and one matching disadvantage: their size. Folded and stored, they present little problem, but to display or play the game a large surface, at least 60 cm (2 ft) square, must be found. Additional space is needed for pieces of equipment – dice, teetotum, counters, booklets and cards. Many of the games are attractive enough to be framed as pictures and this is one way to display many, so long as the framing materials used are not harmful.

It is important to remember that games were initially produced to be fun and to be enjoyed. They should remain that way, even though they may now be collected for their aesthetic qualities.

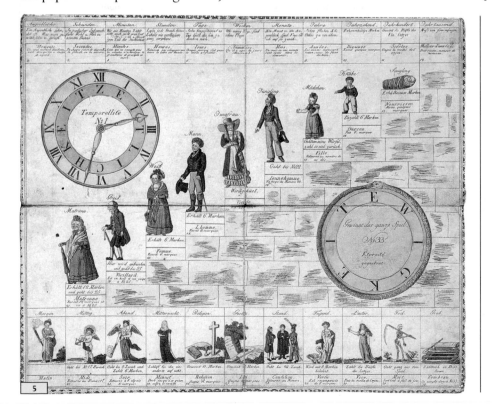

5

Le Grand Terme ou le Jeu des Temps was published in Germany in about 1830 (see also page 51).

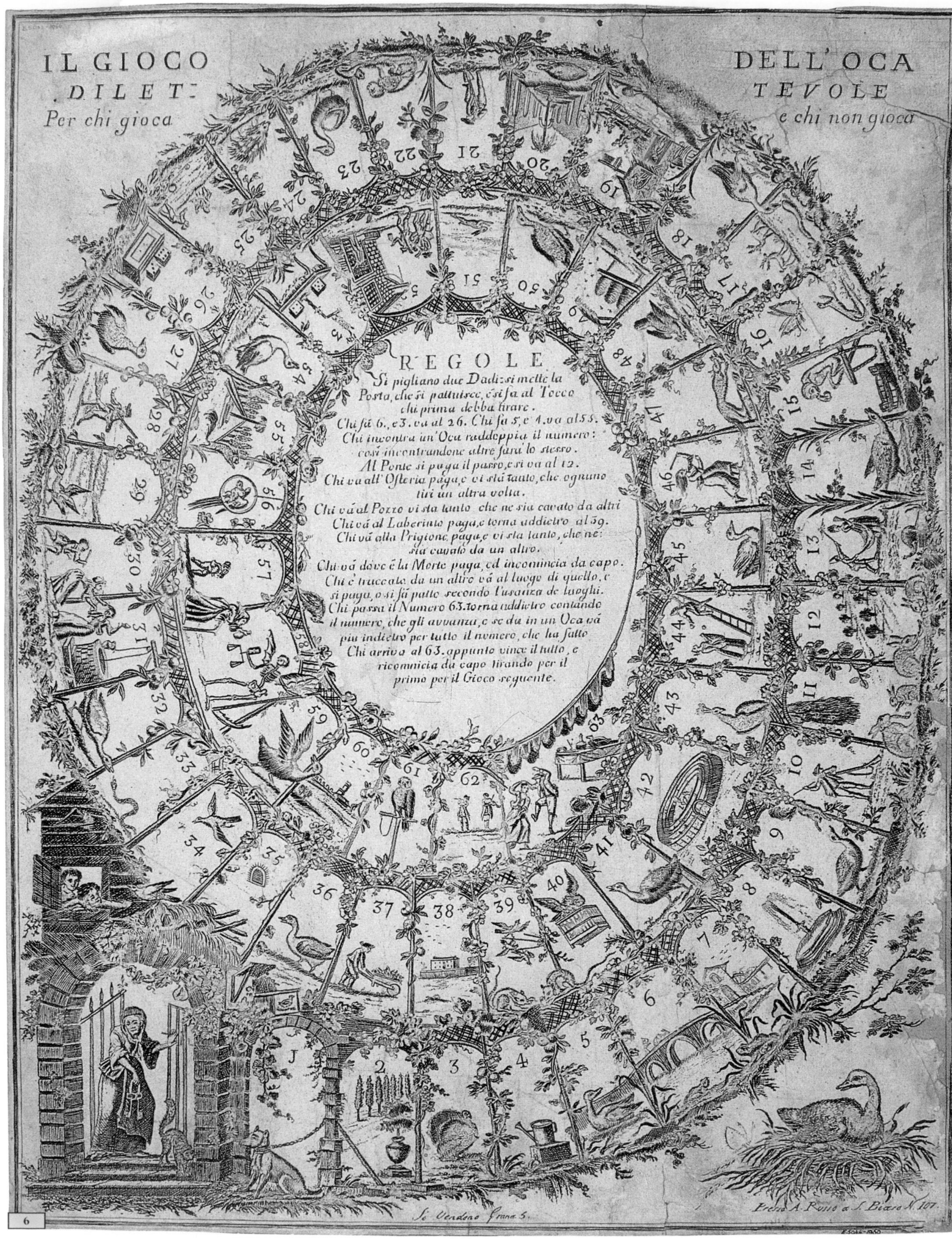

IL GIOCO
DILET:
Per chi gioca

DELL'OCA
TEVOLE
e chi non gioca

REGOLE

Si pigliano due Dadi: si mette la
Posta, che si pattuisce, e si fa al Tocco
chi prima debba tirare.
Chi fa 6., e 3. va al 26. Chi fa 5, e 4. va al 53.
Chi incontra un'Oca raddoppia il numero:
così incontrandone altre farà lo stesso.
Al Ponte si paga il passo, e si va al 12.
Chi va all'Osteria paga, e vi sta tanto, che ognuno
tiri un'altra volta.
Chi và al Pozzo vi sta tanto, che ne sia cavato da altri
Chi và al Laberinto paga, e torna addietro al 39.
Chi và alla Prigione, paga, e vi sta tanto, che ne
sia cavato da un altro.
Chi và dove è la Morte paga, ed incomincia da capo.
Chi è truccato da un altro và al luogo di quello, e
si paga, o si fa patto secondo l'usanza de luoghi.
Chi passa il Numero 63. torna addietro contando
il numero, che gli avvanza, e se da in un Oca và
più indietro per tutto il numero, che ha fatto
Chi arriva al 63. appunto vince il tutto, e
ricomincia da capo tirando per il
primo per il Gioco seguente.

Se Verdino Grana 5.

Presso A. Rosso a S. Biaso N. 107.

RACE GAMES

Games for two or more players tend to be race games in which the object is to achieve a win but in which there is an element of chance. Race games are often gambling games: it is usual to have a central pool, or kitty, into which all players place an agreed number of counters as a stake. Throughout a game, rewards are given and penalties paid by either taking a counter from or putting a counter in to the kitty. Other forms of rewards and forfeits may be used alongside this system, notably moving backwards or forwards or missing turns, and occasionally players pay counters to each other. In race games players' markers are not removed from the board although in some games, when two land on the same square, they change places.

Why was it that this game format produced such a wealth of educational games, including those teaching morals and behaviour, even though they retained the element of gambling and chance? Quite simply, they were exciting to play. Astute publishers could use this characteristic to great advantage to encourage learning and skills.

THE GAME OF THE GOOSE

The *Game of the Goose* is generally regarded as the prototype of the modern race game. Devised in Italy and probably based on games seen in the Middle and Far East, it is said to have been a gift from Francesco de Medici of Florence to King Philip II of Spain between 1574 and 1587. The game spread throughout Europe and it was registered in London in June, 1597 by John Wolfe as '. . . the Newe and Most Pleasant Game of the Goose.'

6

Il Gioco Dell'Oca Dilettevole, (The Pleasing Game of the Goose), an Italian engraving of the mid 18th century, has 63 illustrated compartments representing a journey. The compartments are arranged in an anti-clockwise spiral with the rules printed in the centre. Along the bottom edge are the words 'Si Vendono Grana, 5 Presso A Rosso a S. Diaso No. 107', the address where the game could be purchased.

7

7

With only 61 compartments but otherwise very similar in design to *Il Gioco Dell'Oca Dilettevole* is a hand-drawn and painted representation of the game, which also closely resembles an early English version of *The Game of the Goose*, published in about 1725 for John Bowles & Son. *The Game of the Goose* was produced in England between 1790 and 1810, and it is, in fact, a sheet of paper, which was hand-drawn and painted, then mounted on a block of wood. The rules are very similar too, with rewards and penalties, and while it was devised to be enjoyed, the game also contains the moralistic elements of good and bad. Landing on a goose allows the player to 'double his chance forward' while if a player lands at the ale house, he or she incurs a double penalty of paying one stake and waiting until all the other players have had a turn. Some penalties are even more severe, death and overthrowing 61 mean that the player has to go back to the beginning again.

8

Laurie's New and Entertaining Game of the Golden Goose has similar rules, but the layout is completely different. The playing surface is in the form of a goose set against a pastoral scene. There are 63 numbered circles, some of which bear illustrations. The hand-coloured engraving, which is composed of 18 individual sheets, is mounted on linen and the set was reissued several times. This particular example was published by Richard Holmes Laurie on November 22, 1831.

PUBLISHERS AND PRINTERS

The **publisher** *is the person or company who brings an item to the public. He is an agent, dealing as a wholesaler or retailer, or in many cases as both. The publisher could also be the originator or creator of a new game.*

The **printer** *is the person or company who physically produces the item. He is not necessarily the originator or creator of a game, but*

he could be. Likewise, the printer and the publisher could be the same person.

There were, of course, artists and designers. Unfortunately the artists generally remain unknown. They worked for the publishers, but in some cases, the publisher, printer and artist was the same person.

Most of the early games bear their publisher's

name and the date of publication. Few bear the printer's name, though that name appears on the booklets which accompanied the games. Copyright laws, established in 1767 to permit exclusive rights, did not necessarily protect the rights and printers and publishers were obliged to wait over a century until such protection came in 1881.

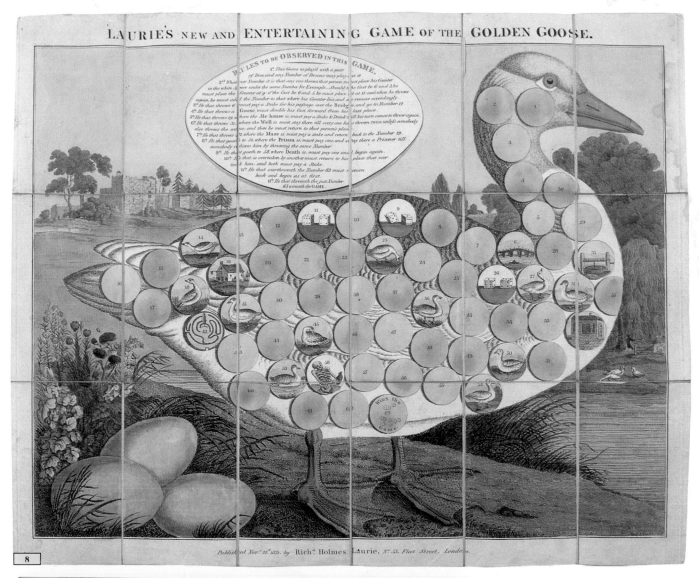

9

9

The Game of the Goose proved to be popular, and many publishers reproduced it, often up to several times. J W Spear & Sons of London, a company that was founded in 1877, designed a format in about 1910 showing children playing. Boards of various sizes were issued including one as recently as 1977. This latest example has goose-shaped markers made of stained wood, whereas the earlier board used cardboard geese mounted on blocks of wood. The rules remain the same, however, and there are 68 compartments. The 1910 issue of *The Game of the Goose* is a chromolithograph published by J W Spear & Sons, London and printed at the company's works in Bavaria, Germany.

Variations on the theme of the goose are numerous, even without including educational games. *The Royal Pastime of Cupid,* or *Entertaining Game of the Snake,* has similar rules and was published by Richard H Laurie in about 1850. This uncoloured engraving may have been taken from a mid-18th century plate produced for

Robert Sayer, a well-established map and print seller, who was succeeded by Robert Laurie and James Whittle in 1794 and by Richard H Laurie in 1813. The ancient Egyptian Game of the Snake, also a spiral pattern, may have inspired many race games, but the rules of this game are not known and they are unlikely to have been the same, although the aim of the game was

the same – to win.

The reissuing of existing and popular games was, often by different publishers, common practice. Often the only changes made were to the names and dates, but occasionally extra compartments were added, such as the updating of an historical game from King George III's period to include Queen Victoria.

LAURIE AND WHITTLE, LONDON

Robert Laurie and James Whittle of London were well-known map and print publishers. Robert Laurie was an engraver working as early as 1779 but, in partnership with James Whittle, acquired the business of Robert Sayer in 1794

whose work they reissued a number of times. Robert Laurie was succeeded by his son, Richard Holmes Laurie, in 1812, and he took over the business totally after James Whittle died in 1818. The address found for both Laurie and Whittle

and R H Whittle was 53 Fleet Street, which was used up to 1859. As was the case with other publishers, they often worked in conjunction with other publishing companies to produce games, notably William Darton.

The New & Favorite Game of MOTHER GOOSE and the GOLDEN EGG.

RULES FOR PLAYING.

1. This Game is played with a Tetotum, marked on 6 sides, and any number of persons may play at it.

2. Each player must be provided with a dozen Counters, (which, before playing, they may value as they please), and a coloured one for a mark.—At the beginning of the Game each player must put 6 into the Pool.

3. Spin for first player, and whoever spins the highest number must begin the Game.

4. Whatever number you spin, place your Mark on that number; and if it be a print, refer to the Explanation.—When it is your turn to spin again, add the two numbers together and move on accordingly.

5. Whoever spins a Golden Egg takes a counter from the Pool; but if you spin a blank, put one in.

6. If two players arrive at the same number, he that was there first is to move back to the place the last player left, from whom he is to receive 1 for resigning his place.

7. Whoever arrives at the exact number (33) first, wins the Game; but if, by spinning, he goes beyond that number, he must move twice as many as he exceeds it.

REFERENCES TO THE GAME.

No. 1. Mother Goose mounted on a Gander.—Pay 4 to secure her favour.

3. Mother Goose's Retreat.

5. Colin receiving the Goose from Mother Goose, who tells him to give the Egg to Avaro, Colinette's Father.—Take up 2.

7. Colin shews the Golden Egg to Avaro, who wants him to kill the Goose, that he may give him all the Eggs at once, before he marries Colinette.

9. Colin, having ungratefully consented to kill the Goose, presented him by his best friend, is changed by Mother Goose to Harlequin, and Colinette to Columbine.—Pay 5 for ingratitude.

11. The mock dance between the Clown, and Harlequin, dressed as a Barrow-Woman.—Stay 1 turn to see this.

13. The Clown and Pantaloon (formerly Avaro) coming to an Inn, they sit down to supper with the Landlord, when Harlequin enters and causes the chairs and tables to ascend with them, while he and Columbine sit down quietly to their supper, laughing at the situation of the others: before they can get down you may move on to No. 18.

15. The Clown and Pantaloon entering in pursuit of Harlequin and Columbine, the former is caught in a Steel Trap, while a Spring-Gun goes off and frightens Pantaloon, who leads off the Clown by the leg.—Pay 2 to have your wound cured.

17. Harlequin and Columbine, to elude pursuit, place themselves as the two well-known figures at St. Dunstan's Church, striking the bell. Take up 4 for this ingenious thought.

No. 19. Vauxhall Gardens, where the Clown gains admission by appearing as a Pandean Minstrel, playing on a fish-kettle with a ladle and whisk, with his chin resting on a hair-broom.—Stay two turns to see the Amusements of the Place, and laugh at this curious figure.

21. The Clown steals a letter from the Post-Office, containing a Bank-Note, which he pockets; then another, in which he finds a small Cord, and these words, "Sir, I'll trouble you with a hint."—For this knavish trick pay 3.

23. The Clown, attempting to drink out of a bottle, finds himself disappointed by the bottom always presenting itself to his lips.—You must be disappointed by going back to No. 14.

25. Harlequin pours wine from his sword into the mouth of Odd Fish. For this act of humanity take up 6.

27. Odd Fish, in gratitude to Harlequin, dives into the Sea after the Golden Egg, which he presents to his benefactor.

29. Harlequin restores the Golden Egg to Mother Goose, who is at length pacified.—Having made some amends for your fault, take up 2.

31. Harlequin and Columbine united by Mother Goose in a Submarine Palace, the dwelling of Odd Fish. This being a most beautiful Scene, you may stay one turn to admire it.

33. An exact representation of Mother Goose mounted on her favorite Gander.—By her permission you are allowed to take all the fish remaining in the Pool, and are declared winner of this Game.

N.B. If the Players are inclined for another Game, the winner of the first is to begin it.

London: Printed for John Wallis, 42, Skinner Street, Snow-Hill, by J. Vevers, 14, York Street, Covent Garden.

Similar rules but with a different story line form the basis of *The New and Favorite Game of Mother Goose and the Golden Egg*, which shows episodes and characters from the pantomime of the same title, including the Clown and Harlequin, and places in London, including St Dunstan's Church and Vauxhall Gardens. Published at the height of the career of Grimaldi the Clown, who is featured in compartment 21, much of the game is taken up with rules, and the number of compartments is reduced to 33, of which 17 are illustrated, each having its own story and reward or forfeit. Half the remaining compartments show a golden egg, which if landed on, has a reward of one counter; the other half, which are blank, carry a forfeit of one counter. This game, a hand-coloured etching, was published by John Wallis on November 30th, 1808.

RACING TO LEARN

As many of the publishers of the early games were already producing maps, the first games tended to be geographical in nature, and often simply used an existing map. According to the booklet which accompanied *Geographical Recreations* or *a Voyage Around the Habitable World* in 1809:

This game, consisting of 116 little prints of the most interesting objects in Geography, is designed to familiarise youth with the names and relative situations of places, together with the manners, customs, and dresses of the different nations in the habitable globe; and, as curiosity will naturally be excited by the scenes which present themselves, and the observations likely to occur, it is presumed that these, with an occasional reference to the Synopsis herewith given, will prove a continual source of amusement to young people of both sexes, and will furnish such a fund of geographical knowledge, as may prove equally beneficial in reading and conversation.

12

A New Royal Geographical Pastime for England and Wales was published in 1787 and bears the secondary title 'Whereby the Distance of each Town is Laid Down from London in Measured Miles Being a very amusing Game to Play with a Teetotum, Ivory Pillars [markers] and Counters.' The game is a hand-coloured engraving in 16 sections mounted on linen and it was published by Robert Sayer on June 1st, 1787. There are 169 principal and county towns joined by lines, and on each side are the rules, listing each of the towns with a short description of it and any rewards to be received or forfeits to be paid. Rewards take the form of extra moves or turns, while the forfeits involve the loss of both moves and turn, and payments. However, there are no charges for moving from one place to another. One of the better rewards occurs at Stonehenge 'worthy of visiting without expense, from whence you are to be removed to Chester at 148.' One of the harshest is at Knaresborough, 163, 'which has four medicinal springs of different qualities; to drink from them you pay 1 counter and are conveyed to Bath, 2.' The game itself is enlightening, for it not only refers to visiting stately homes, cathedrals, churches and other public buildings but also describes events, folklore and geographical features such as smuggling, the flitch of bacon given at Dunmow and the Giant's Causeway.

ROBERT SAYER, LONDON

Working at 53 Fleet Street, Robert Sayer was one of the first and leading publishers of material for children, publishing both games and puzzles. Starting in 1745, with his business being sold to Laurie and Whittle in 1794, *Sayer produced many educational games, which were mostly in the form of maps, but he also produced a* Game of the Goose *and the* Game of the Snake *which were later reissued by Laurie and Whittle.*

13

Royal Geographical Amusement of the Safe and Expeditious Traveller Through all the Parts of Europe by Sea and by Land, a hand-coloured engraving, was published by Richard Holmes Laurie on December 1, 1823. This game was originally a companion to *A New Royal Geographical Pastime for England and Wales*, which was published by Robert Sayer, and its sheet of rules still bears Sayer's name. The secondary title of this game reveals the true purpose for which it was designed: *An Instructive Game Calculated for the Improvement of the Young Learners of Geography by Dr Journey.*

14

Wallis's Tour Through England and Wales, a New Geographical Pastime was published by John Wallis on December 24th, 1794 and was a hand-coloured engraving in 16 sections mounted on linen. Like *A New Royal Geographical Pastime for England and Wales*, the towns and descriptions are shown together with any rewards or penalties, but in this case there are only 117 compartments. Although the basic playing method is the same, there is one major difference and that is the kitty. To start, each player has a marker, called a traveller, and four counters, which are kept. Most of the forfeits involve missing turns, but two ask for payment. The Isle of Man is the harshest. There the traveller is shipwrecked and has to leave the game. The descriptions of the towns, while still creating the illusion of a visit to an interesting place, highlight the idea of commerce and trade. Many manufacturing towns are mentioned, including Worcester for its china and gloves, Manchester and Leeds for their cloths, and Berwick for its salmon fisheries. This game continued to be available for many years, and the rules booklet for this example was printed in 1802.

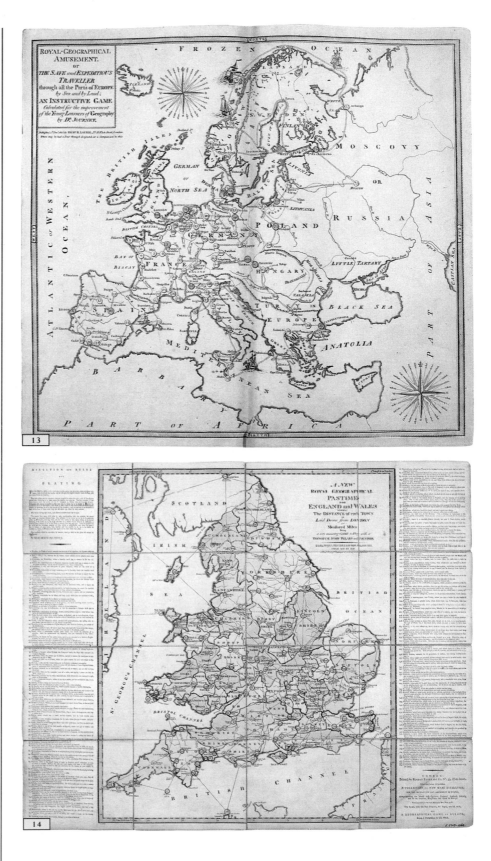

21

15

Wallis produced a companion *Tour of Europe* which was also published in 1794 and it bears the date November 24th, 1794. Likewise it was a hand-coloured engraving in 16 sections mounted on linen. This shows 102 towns, some of which were capitals of the 'kingdoms and states' of Europe, and landing on one of these brings the privilege of doubling the last spin. Most of the descriptions stress what might be seen in each town, and some reflect military activities such as battles, arsenals and fortifications. Both the *Tour of England and Wales* and the *Tour of Europe* give an insight into what was currently regarded as historically and commercially important. Of course, these games were published at the height of the Grand Tour of Europe, and all that was thought to be best was included.

JOHN HARRIS, LONDON

John Harris took over the publishing firm of Elizabeth Newbery in 1801. He primarily produced games, but did make a few dissected puzzles. His address was the same as Newbery's, Corner of St Paul's Churchyard, with the title 'Original Juvenile Library'. In 1843 Harris sold his business to Grant & Griffith. Some of Harris's publications were issued in conjunction with John Wallis.

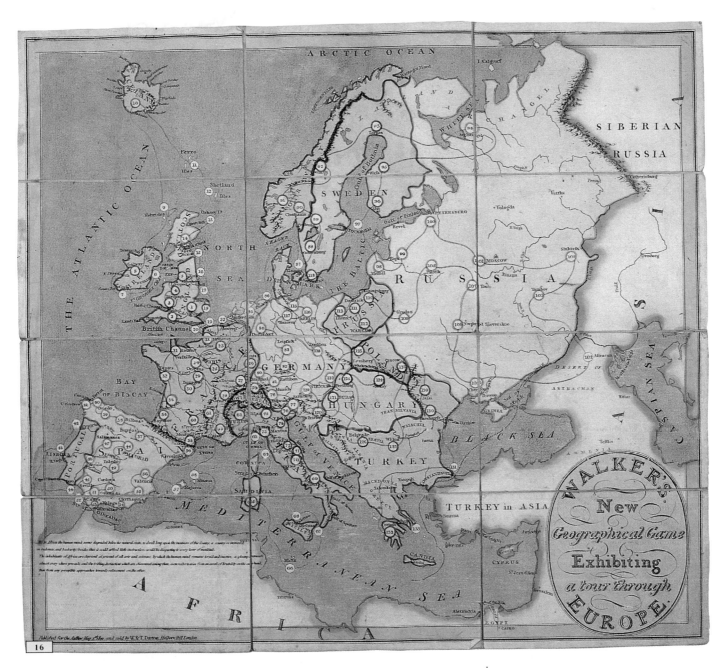

16

Walker's New Geographical Game Exhibiting a Tour Throughout Europe, is played in a similar manner to Wallis's Tour of Europe and was a hand-coloured engraving mounted on linen, published by W & T Darton for the author, Walker, on May 1st, 1810. It shows the capitals, major cities and major sea routes of Europe, and the accompanying rules booklet gives detailed descriptions and the rewards or forfeits for each. As with the other games, great emphasis is placed on the geographical and historical element together with commerce. The booklets used a wide vocabulary, and, as the games were devised for children under the age of 12, they not only provided knowledge but also encouraged reading and speaking skills.

17

Round the World with Nellie Bly, copyrighted by J A Crozier in 1890, is a race game described as 'A Novel and Fascinating Game of Excitement on Land and See'. It also bears the copyright date 1904 and was produced for many years by McLoughlin Brothers. Nellie Bly was in fact an investigative journalist whose real name was Elizabeth Cochrane Seaman. In 1889/90, she travelled around the world in 72 days, 6 hours and 11 minutes thus beating the time of Phileas Fogg, the hero of Jules Verne's novel *Around the World in Eighty Days.*

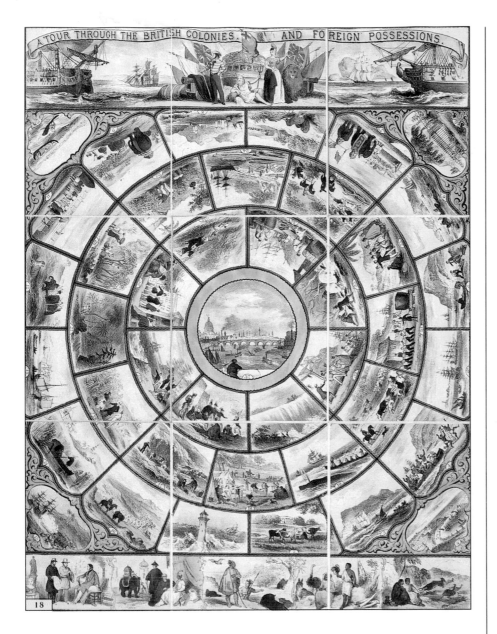

18

19

19

India and other places mentioned in *A Tour Through The British Colonies and Foreign Possessions* also feature in William Sallis's *Dioramic Game of the Overland Route to India*, a coloured lithograph published in about 1850. Again, long and detailed descriptions are given as well as directions of play in the accompanying booklet, although this time the players start from Southampton Docks and finish in Calcutta.

18

In many of the older geographical games, London is the centre from which the players leave or to which they return. In his game *A Tour Through the British Colonies and Foreign Possessions*, a hand-coloured lithograph published in about 1850, John Betts calls London the metropolis of the British Empire. The other 36 stops are well documented in a rules booklet, and their descriptions, as part of the game, must be read out. Interestingly two routes to India are provided, one overland via Alexandria, which is mentioned as being important even though it is not a colony, and the other via Sierre Leone and the Cape. It is perhaps surprising to presentday readers to see how well informed and up-to-date some of the comments are – disapproval of the selling of gunpowder and spirits to North American Indians and the fact that Newfoundland was 'rediscovered' by Sebastian Cabot in 1496, for example. With the booklet is an extensive catalogue of the other games and amusements issued by Betts. These were largely educational and included scriptural puzzles, mathematical, scientific and spelling games as well as a wide range of maps.

20

The mysteries of the Orient, discovered through the use of an imaginative illustration, are to be found in *The Noble Game of the Elephant and Castle* or *Travelling in Asia*, published by William Darton in 1822. This game definitely stresses learning through reading, as the booklet has 84 pages of text to accompany the 24 compartments shown on this hand-coloured engraving.

21

Using the race game format and a map of the United States, McLoughlin Brothers copyrighted the *Game of Uncle Sam's Mail* in 1893. The lithographed box label shows various methods of transporting mail from one side of the country to the other and the aim of the game is to be the first to reach one's destination while learning a great deal about the country itself.

22

The mysteries of the Orient were popular themes in other countries too, perhaps the countries were studying each other. Published in 1903 by a less well known American company was the *Game of Japan*. It was issued by the lithography company Ottoman Litho of New York City which produced a number of inexpensive games priced between 25c and $1.00.

21

23

23

An interesting double sided wooden puzzle, which used the original term 'dissected' in its descriptive title, showed a map of New York State. Published in the 1890s under the series name Silent Teacher by C E Hartman of Utica, NY, it describes Hartman as the 'Successor of Rev. E J Clemens' and as a 'Manufacturer of Dissected Maps', thus following the tradition of the English map dissectors begun a century before. Silent Teacher puzzles were first issued by the Union Sectional Map Company in the 1870s and by the 1880s Rev. E J Clemens was operating the business. During the 1890s Hartman was in control.

24

24

In the 1930s Parker Brothers produced a geographical game which was also based on the adventures of Admiral Byrd and his visit to the South Pole. The title is fairly obvious, *Admiral Byrd's South Pole Game 'Little America',* but the game itself reflects all the modern telecommunications and transport of the day.

25

Also published in 1928 was *The Game of the World Flyers Air Race, Around the World Flight.* 'An-All-Fair-Game', produced by the Alderman, Fairchild Company, uses model aircraft as the playing pieces and each player follows his own coloured path around the board. The moves are determined by a simmer or dice and directions are printed on the game squares. Moves forward and backward and missed turns are all part of the forfeits and rewards of this game.

25

HISTORY MADE EASY

The British games teaching geography, although essentially looking at the world from a British viewpoint, were prepared to acknowledge that other places and people might be interesting and worthwhile. However, the games designed to teach history were much more inward looking and were strictly based on events as they affected the British Isles. During the period when most of these games were published, George III was king (1760–1820) and he became the focal point of the games, whether the events occurred in his lifetime or not. If the games are studied without any prior knowledge, one would be led to the conclusion that Britain and its people did not exist before 1066, as most start with the Battle of Hastings and William the Conqueror.

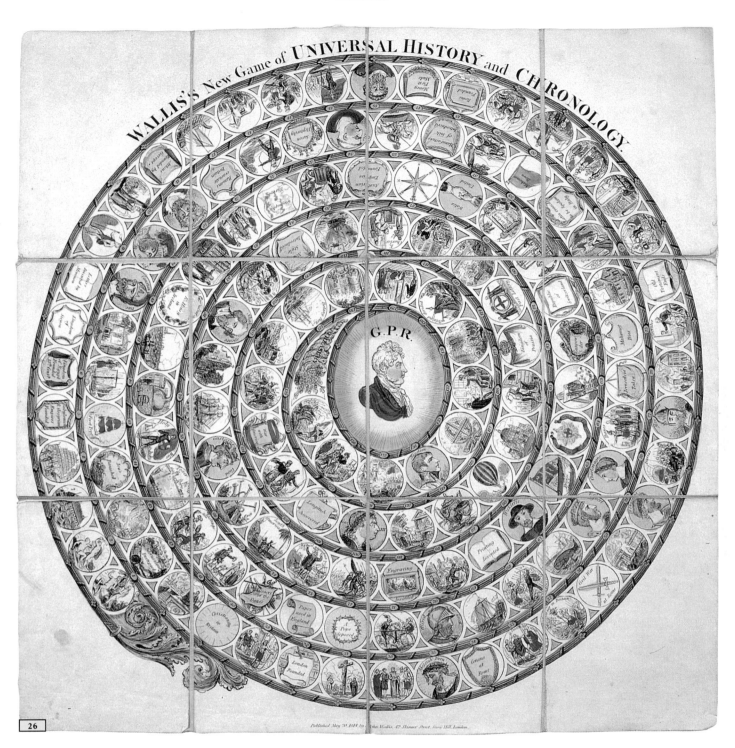

26

Published May 20, 1814, by John Wallis, 42 Skinner Street, Snow Hill, London.

26

A few games do, however, begin with Adam and Eve. Out of the 138 compartments illustrated on John Wallis's *New Game of Universal History and Chronology*, the first 75 are devoted to events before 1066. Each compartment has a date, starting at Anno Mundi 1 and all the dates are given with such conviction – for example, the Universal Deluge occurred in AM 1636 – that one wonders if this knowledge was lost between 1814 and today. In the centre is George, Prince Regent (later King George IV). A reworked impression of this game was published in about 1840, and had five compartments replacing the portrait. Among the new subjects were King William IV and Queen Victoria, the marriage of Queen Victoria, and a railway train. Both versions of the game were hand-coloured. The rules booklet that accompanied the earlier example gave brief descriptions of each compartment and some directions, and at the end of the booklet were longer descriptions of some of the subjects, which had to be read aloud if a player landed on the revelant number. The game was a hand-coloured engraving published by John Wallis on May 20th, 1814.

27

The starting compartment of Wallis's *New Game of Universal History and Chronology*, whether of the 1814 or the 1840 issue, has an illustration of Adam and Eve.

28

Whereas the finishing compartment in the centre of the 1814 issue bears a portrait of George, Prince Regent pictured here, the centre of the reworked issue of the game is quite different, showing five small compartments instead of the portrait.

29

Reducing the period covered allowed the publishers to go into greater detail about the history that they and the buying public felt had determined their country. On December 1st, 1803 John Harris, in conjunction with John Wallis, published *Historical Pastimes* or *A New Game of the History of England*. It shows 158 medallions representing all types of events and characters, each of which is listed in the accompanying rules booklet together with directions of play. Also in the booklet are details of all the kings and queens from William I to George III. In this game, which is an engraving, the medallions are painted in one of four colours – blue, pink, green or yellow – rather than being highlighted with appropriate colours.

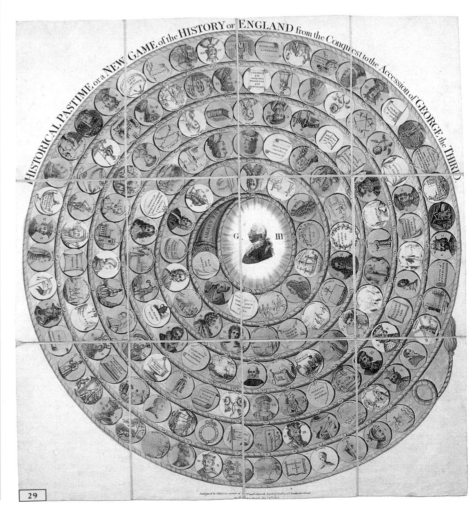

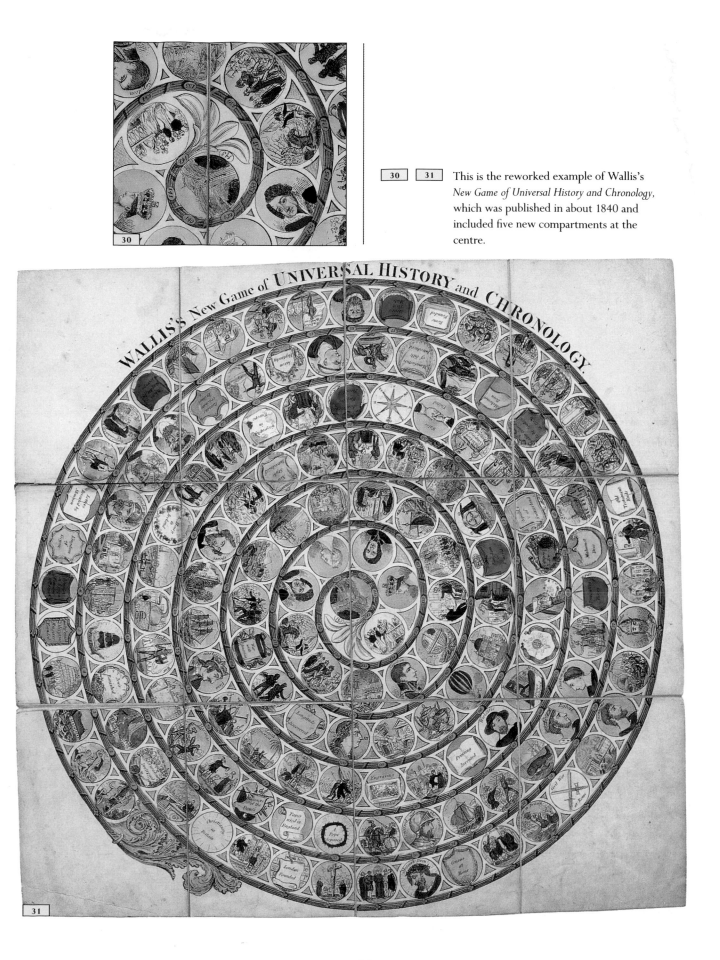

30 31 This is the reworked example of Wallis's *New Game of Universal History and Chronology*, which was published in about 1840 and included five new compartments at the centre.

32

32

An updated and reworked version of *Historical Pastimes* or *A New Game of the History of England* was published in 1828. A few alterations included the main central picture which was changed to show King George IV. This game, like its earlier version, has the medallions painted in one of four colours – blue, pink, green and yellow – rather than highlighting each with appropriate colours.

33

33

Published by John Harris in 1810, the centre compartment of the hand-coloured engraving *The Jubilee* has a portrait of King George III.

34

As with *Historical Pastimes*, each of the 150 compartments of *The Jubilee* is detailed, and there is a further text listing, year by year, the events considered important. This text, which uses flowery language in praise of the king, does not refrain from describing some of the more disagreeable events. It also includes descriptions of scientific and geographical discoveries. Each scene is highlighted in a wide range of colours.

34

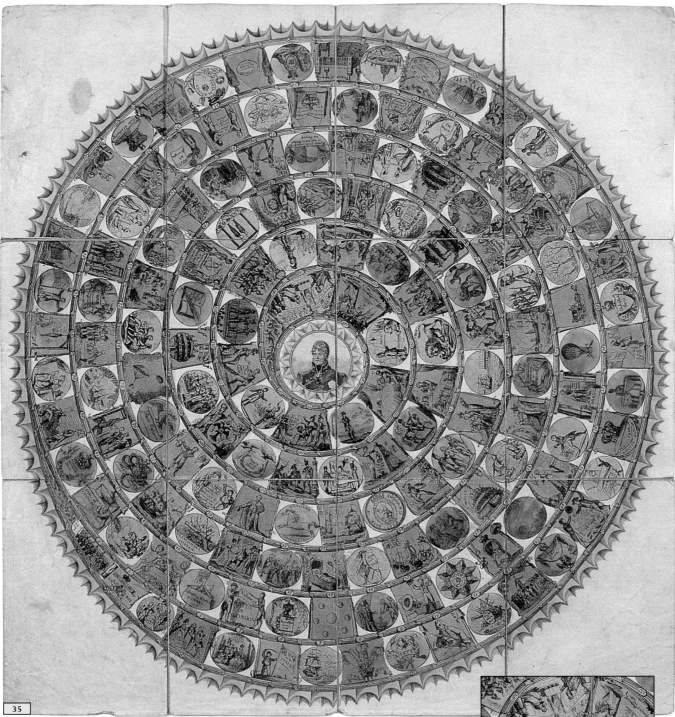

35

35

A reworked impression of the game, *The Jubilee*, was published 10 years later with the title *The Sun of Brunswick*. It is a hand-coloured etching which was published by John Harris on May 1st, 1820 but the treatment of its compartments is entirely different from that of the early game. Each compartment is painted with one of four colours – blue, pink, green or yellow.

36

The centre of the game, *The Sun of Brunswick*, has been reworked. Compartments 129 to 150 were amended to include the deaths of Queen Charlotte, the wife of King George III, Charlotte Augusta, Princess of Wales, the daughter of King George IV and heir apparent to the throne, and of King George III himself.

36

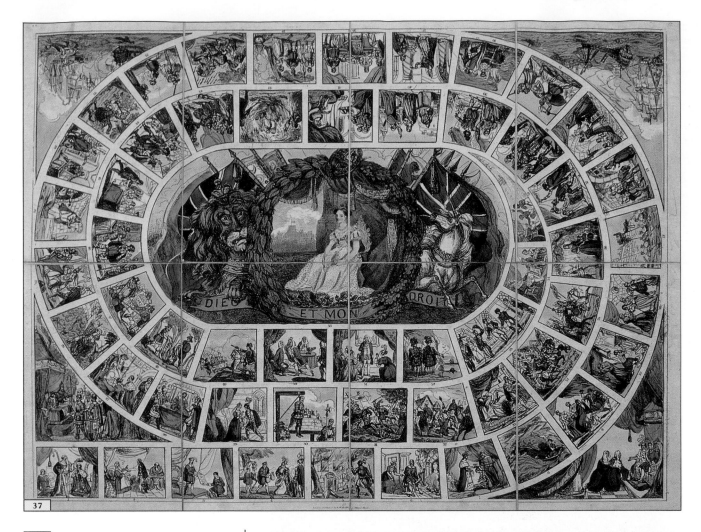

37

37

The last of the board games reflecting English history were published at the beginning of the reign of Queen Victoria. Dramatic social changes were taking place, and the idea of teaching through this form of play was quickly falling from favour. Nevertheless, with the accession of the new queen in 1837, a number of games, updated to include her coronation and marriage, were issued in about 1840. *British Sovereigns* was published by John Passmore and Edward Wallis in about 1840 and included portraits of British kings and queens starting with Egbert.

38

Amusement in English History, published by William Sallis in about 1840, also showed events that had taken place before the reign of King William I. *British Sovereigns* and *Amusement in English History* have a different format from earlier games and fewer scenes.

38

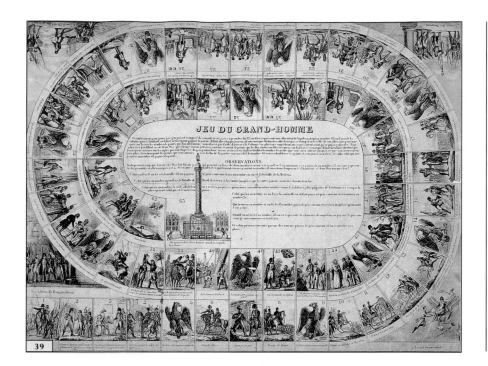

39

Games relating to history and geography were, of course, not confined to England. *Jeu du Grand-Homme*, which has 63 numbered compartments and four pictorial corners, celebrates the important events in the life of Napoleon I. The game was published by Veuve Turgot of Paris c.1835.

40

Jeu Des Monuments de Paris, which is similarly arranged as *Jeu du Grand-Homme* and published *c* 1835, shows places of great interest in the city. The rules of both games are in the centre.

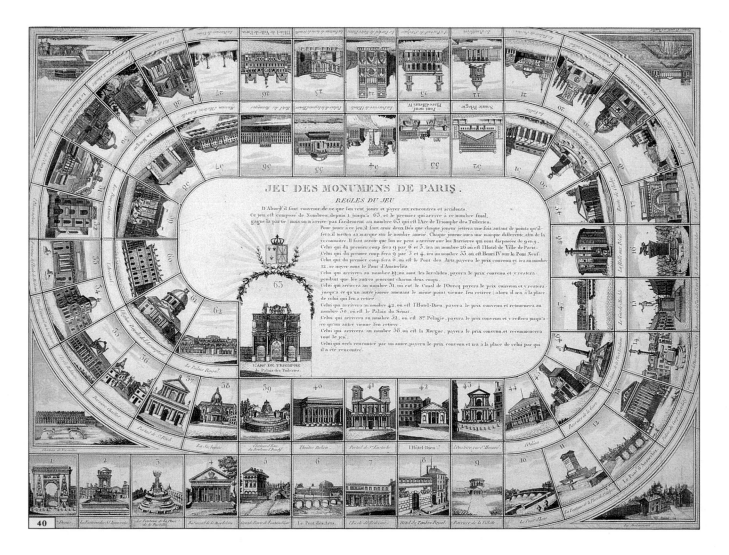

THE THREE R'S PLUS

The final educational use of these early race games was to teach a range of subjects such as mathematics, natural history and languages. The games themselves were sometimes less exciting to play or even to look at but, if played correctly, they were enjoyable ways of learning.

41

41

Published on December 15th, 1791 by C Taylor was a game for teaching mathematics. The game is a hand-coloured engraving titled *An Arithmetical Pastime*. There are 100 circles, some of which contain illustrations while others have directions and forfeits. The forfeits refer to repeating certain tables, some of which are obvious – the times table, for example – some less so – the wine measure table, for instance – while others, such as the avoirdupois table (the weights table of ounces and pounds), are obscure today. In the corners are the addition, subtraction, multiplication and division tables and directions for their use. If a player could not pay the forfeit he or she had the choice of missing turns or moving backwards.

The same game was issued in 1798 by John Wallis. Thereafter *An Arithmetical Pastime* had quite different rules. Two teetotums were required to learn the mathematical disciplines. The players subtracted the number shown on one teetotum from the number on the other (whichever was greatest), or multiplied the two numbers shown and used the last number of the result for their move, or divided the two numbers and used the result plus the remainder for their move. Used in parallel with these directions were the compartments on the playing sheet. Each had an accompanying verse to be read out and further rewards or forfeits. This was a game that could teach everything – morals, history, geography and arithmetic.

42

Closely linked with the mathematical games are those that relate to astronomy. *Science in Sport* or *The Pleasures of Astronomy*, was published by John Wallis in 1804. The 35 compartments have portraits of astronomers and representations of astronomical phenomena. At the time, nine planets and their movements around the sun were known. Intermingled with facts are compartments dealing with fiction (the Man in the Moon) behaviour (the Studious Boy and the Blockhead), signs of the zodiac, comets and rainbows, and astronomers. This game, a hand-coloured engraving mounted on linen, was issued later by Edward Wallis.

42

43

43

Covering a wide range of subjects which are arranged in a pattern of three compartments every 16th place, is the *Circle of Knowledge*, published in about 1845 by John Passmore. The game is laid out in four concentric circles; three contain 16 pictures and the inner ring shows the signs of the zodiac and the four cardinal points of the compass. For example, Europe is illustrated in compartments 1, 17 and 33 while Asia is shown in 5, 21 and 37. Africa and America are also shown, as are the four seasons, the four houses of the zodiac and the four sciences – electricity, chemistry, optics and astronomy. The illustrations are quite unusual – fire, for instance, is illustrated by a volcano, a burning farm and a pit explosion, and optics is represented by a giant telescope, a magic lantern show and the perspective of a tunnel.

44

Published in 1820 by William Darton is perhaps one of the best games about natural history, *British and Foreign Animals*, which has the subtitle 'A New Game, Moral, Instructive and Amusing, designed to allure the Minds of Youth to an Acquaintance with the Wonders of Nature'. The 56-page booklet describes each animal at length and furnishes the player with many facts that still hold true today. Both domestic and wild animals, from all continents, including Australia (the Kangaroo) are discussed. Some directions for play and the forfeits and rewards are given in the text, but it appears that the publisher's overwhelming desire was to instruct children.

44

45

45

The hand-coloured engraving of the game *British and Foreign Animals* was mounted on linen. When not in use, the game was folded up and placed together with its descriptive booklet, which is dated 1820, in a cardboard slip-case which bears a very elaborate engraved label.

46 WILLIAM DARTON, 58, HOLBORN HILL, 1822.

A companion game to *British and Foreign Animals* which was also published by William Darton, in 1822, has the fanciful name *The Delicious Game of the Fruit Basket* or *The Novel and Elegant Game of the Basket of Fruit*. The only reference to fruit is the hand-coloured engraved illustration, as this is strictly a game designed to teach morals by using British institutions as the guidelines. It is of interest as many diverse categories are described, including penitentiaries and trial by jury, the Royal Academy, hospitals, national schools and the School for the Blind, various sciences and religion. Each bears its own reward or forfeit, but the main aim of the game is to encourage learning and reading, rather than to win.

From the middle of the 19th century, other forms of games, notably card games, gradually replaced the educational race games. However, not all the games published between 1770 and 1850 were strictly educational; some were designed to be played for fun or interest. A French game, published in 1778 by Crépy of Paris, illustrated women's hairstyles and costumes. The playing surface, an engraving, has 63 numbered compartments, each showing the head or full-length figure of a lady. In each corner is a scene for a different time of day and the rules are in the centre. As the title states, this game was 'dedicated to the beautiful sex'.

48

A game for five players, published in 1836 by William Darton, uses an imaginary seascape to illustrate the dangers and incidents likely to befall sailors. Each player follows his own course, and directions for moving are indicated by a five-pointed compass. The game, a hand-coloured engraving, has a rather whimsical title, *A Voyage of Discovery* or *The Five Navigators*.

49

The Regatta, a hand-coloured lithograph, was published in England in about 1850 by an unknown company. It is another fanciful sailing game, but based upon the Isle of Wight and showing The Solent and Spithead, various ships and shipping.

RACING AND EDUCATION
IN THE 20TH CENTURY

By the beginning of the 20th century there had been a
revival in educational games, although few had such
strict rules as earlier ones. Many combined good
intentions with fanciful themes.

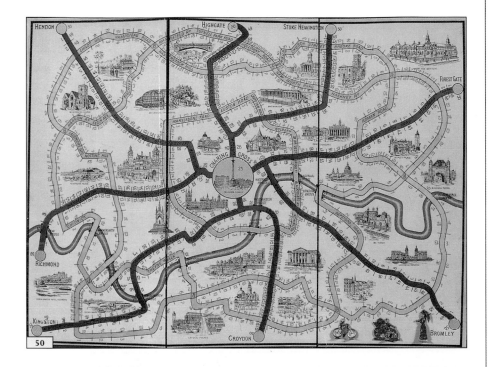

50

Round the Town was designed in England as
part of the Globe Series and printed by
chromolithography in Bavaria between
1900 and 1910. The game has six painted
lead markers in the form of cars, bicycles
and people; these were probably cast by
Britains Ltd, the company famous for its
lead toy soldiers. The playing surface shows
a number of well-known areas of London,
and the game was completed by two bone
dice.

51

Using a very similar game format to *A
Cycling Game* was one published by Milton
Bradley in 1922. A 1920s American slang
term a cheap motorcar or aeroplane has
been used as the title for the *Flivver Game*.
This board game has lead car playing pieces
and a pair of very unusual spinners. The
wheels of the 'flivver' illustrated on a large
card are the spinners which determine the
players' moves. The players' progress across
the board is regulated by instructions
printed on many of the squares.

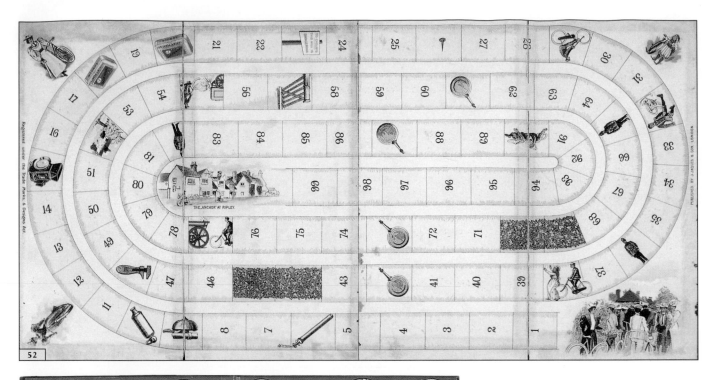

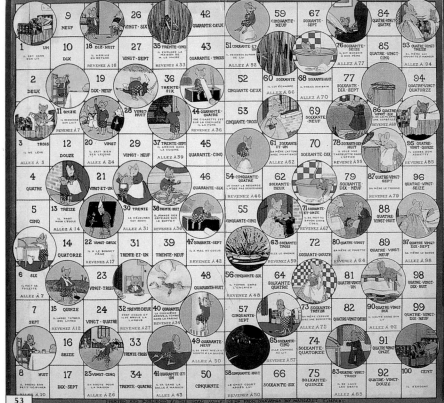

52

Wheeling was published by J Jaques & Son at the beginning of the 20th century and was printed by chromolithography. This game, which also has lead markers in the shape of cyclists, is subtitled *A New and Exciting Game for Cyclists.* It shows many of the adventures and mishaps that befall bicycle riders.

53

Games to teach languages, especially foreign games, are usually found as card games, but board games were sometimes made for this purpose. *La Journee d'un Souriceau (The Day's Doings of a Little Mouse)* uses drawings by Margaret Tempest. All the directions and numbers are in French and the subtitle states that it is 'An Amusing Game for Learning French'. The game was produced as a chromolithograph by The Chad Valley Company of Birmingham in 1924.

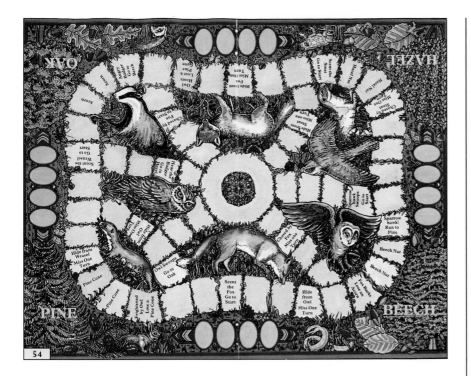

54

A wood mouse, together with a red squirrel, a bank vole and a harvest mouse are featured in *The Wild Wood*, a recently produced game. It requires the players to gather winter stores for the animals and attempts to instil knowledge about the lifestyles of these small woodland inhabitants. The *Wild Wood* was published for the National Trust by Squirrel Publishing in 1984 and was designed by Bob Westley.

GAMES OF FUN

In the 20th century many board games have been produced purely for fun. They are, however, often based on well-known literary characters, people, and events, and among these are two that appeared in the 1930s based on favourite children's story book characters, Peter Rabbit and Winnie the Pooh.

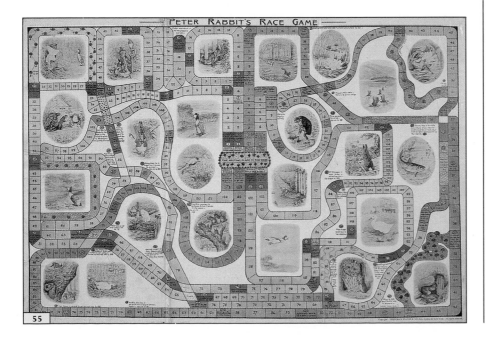

55

55

Peter Rabbit's Race Game was designed for four players, each of whom travels along one of the paths, experiencing adventures along the way. The subtitle states that it is 'an exciting board game introducing Beatrix Potter's world famed characters, Peter Rabbit, Squirrel Nutkin, Jeremy Fisher and Jemima Puddle Duck'. The game, a chromolithograph, was published by Frederick Warne & Co Ltd of London in about 1930. The company, of course, also published the books on which the characters were based.

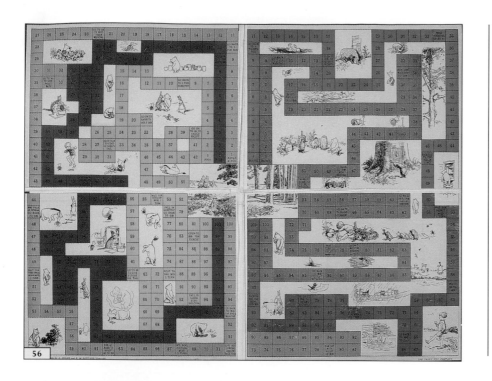

56

Winnie The Pooh's Race Game is naturally very similar in format to *Peter Rabbit's Race Game*. It shows some of the adventures that may be found in the books by A A Milne, although it is less attractive as its colours are brighter. The game was printed by chromolithography and published by the Teddy Toy Company of London in 1935. Both *Winnie the Pooh's Race Game* and that of Peter Rabbit are played with dice and the only goal is to win.

58

The label on the box which contains the game *Little Noddy's Train Game* is far more appealing to a child's eye than most of its predecessors, being brighter and simpler.

57

Little Noddy's Train Game was based on the work of Enid Blyton. It uses the four-track format, with each player having a plastic marker in the shape of a railway engine, of a colour to match the track. The spinner, which shows the numbers 1 to 6, also has a division that can send the player back three spaces. This is in addition to any moves allocated on the board itself. The game was played on a chromolithographed board which was published by the B & S Company of London under the tradename BeStime. It was advertised as 'new' in October 1957.

59

Sometimes the games were based upon nursery rhymes and designed for young children. This was the case for the game *Hickory, Dickory Dock* published by Parker Brothers in 1900. The playing surface is actually on the inside of the bottom of the box. The moves are determined by a spinner which is marked from 1 to 6. The cats illustrated on the lid are very reminiscent of cats available as soft toys printed at the same time by American companies. Some of these designs are being reprinted today.

60

Hollywood itself had no real effect on games, but the studios, films and events did. Walt Disney Productions licensed many of its cartoon characters to become games of one kind or another. The full length cartoon, *Sleeping Beauty*, was one. The players are the Princes who set out to awaken Sleeping Beauty. As it is necessary to enter some of the compartments with exact scores, the spinner has some numbers twice as well as a Good Fairy and a Wicked Fairy. At one point, to enhance the thrill of the game, two paths are offered, one short and dangerous, the other long but safe. The game was published in England by Bell Ltd of London and copyrighted in 1959.

61

Oscar was published in the 1950s by an unknown publisher. The game shows illustrations of well-known stars and represents the fight to gain the coveted award.

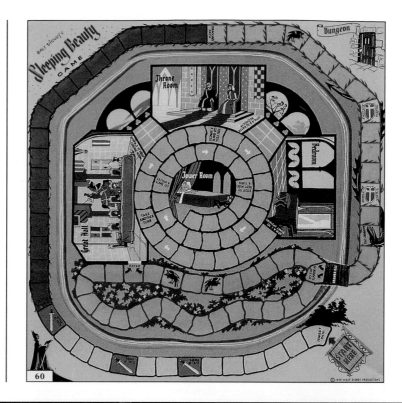

GAMES OF MORALS

THE GOOD AND BAD IN ALL OF US

'Designed for the Amusement of Youth of both Sexes and Calculated to Inspire their Minds with an Abhorrence of Vice and a Love of Virtue,' this subtitle of *The New Game of Emulation*, published in 1804, leaves the players of the following games in no doubt as to the aims of games of morals.

To teach 'morals', publishers used the same format as the race games but employed two distinct methods. One system was based on the progression through life from infancy to old age and all the temptations that might be met along the way. Games in this group generally had the straightforward title *The Game of Human Life*. The second type tended to appear later, and they were more strictly aimed at children, reinforcing the idea that, if you are good you are rewarded, and if you are not, you are punished. These games had much more fanciful names – *The Cottage of Content*, *The Mansion of Happiness* or *The*

Mansion of Bliss, and that good old stand-by, *Virtue Rewarded and Vice Punished,* leaving no one in any doubt as to its purpose.

The rules of play were similar to those of the other race-cum-educational games, with a pool or kitty, a dice or teetotum, and markers and counters. Rewards and forfeits of all kinds were used, some harsher than others. As these games were designed to teach morals, many introduced one significant change – the use of a teetotum instead of dice. Teetotums, which served the same purpose as dice, were small spinning tops with the bulbous part cut to form an even number of sides. The usual number was six, but some had four while others had as many as 12. Each side would bear a number or letter. The rules of *The New Game of Human Life*, which was published in 1790, include the caution: 'It is necessary to inform the Purchaser the Totum must be marked with the figures 1–6 and to avoid introducing a dice box into private Families, each player must spin twice, which will answer the same purpose.'

62

Virtue Rewarded and Vice Punished, published by William Darton in 1820 (see page 55).

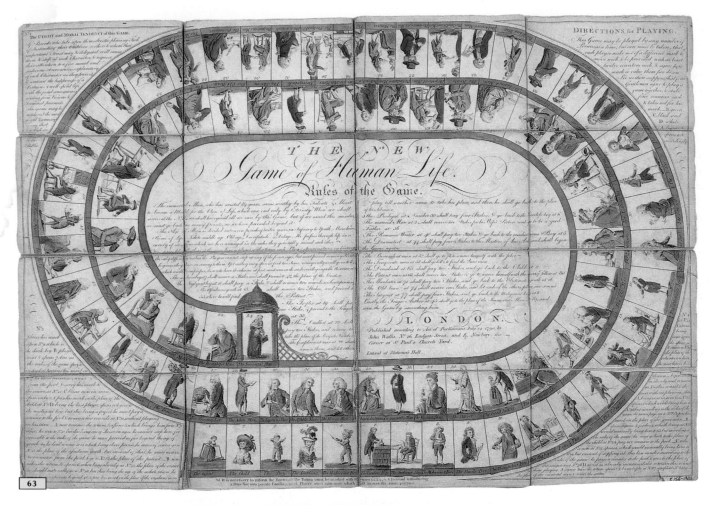

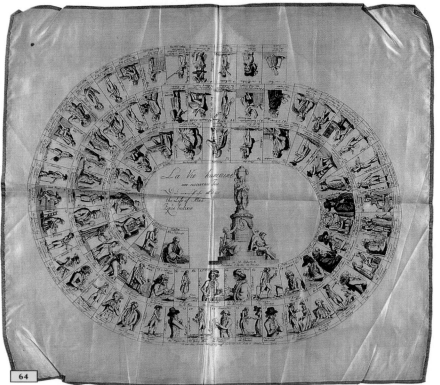

64

Almost identical to *The New Game of Human Life* and dating from the same period, is the German-produced game *La Vie Humaine*, published by Simon Schropp of Berlin in about 1790 and printed on a panel of silk. All the titles are in four languages – French, German, English and Polish – and all but the last illustration are reverse images of Wallis's game. The last image shows a memorial tablet and bust, possibly of Leopold, Prince of Brunswick, (1752–85).

65

A second German game, also with a French title and also showing the ages of man, was *Le Grand Terme ou Le Jeu des Temps*, a hand-coloured etching published in about 1830. This has a completely different format from the others, and the titles are in French and German only. However, it is played in the same manner, with forfeits and rewards and a central kitty.

63

Although it shows the Ages of Man, divided into seven periods of 12 years, *The New Game of Human Life* was not restricted to boys alone as the title reveals: '. . . most Agreeable and Rational Recreation ever Invented for Youth of Both Sexes.' Under the heading 'Utility and Moral Tendency of this Game', the parents are urged to instruct their children on each of the characters with 'a few moral and judicious observations . . . and contrast the happiness of a virtuous and well-spent life with the fatal consequences arising from vicious and immoral pursuits'. Most of the names of the characters have the same meanings today, although some of the punishments accorded would not be considered necessary today, notably those for the authors. The Romance Writer must pay two stakes and return to the Mischievous Boy at 5, while the Dramatist must pay four and begin the game again. The Tragic Author has possibly the harshest penalty, for he goes from 45 to 84, the Immortal Man, and dies; by this move, however, the player actually wins the game and the kitty. *The New Game of Human Life,* a hand-coloured engraving, was published by John Wallis and Elizabeth Newbery on July 29th, 1790.

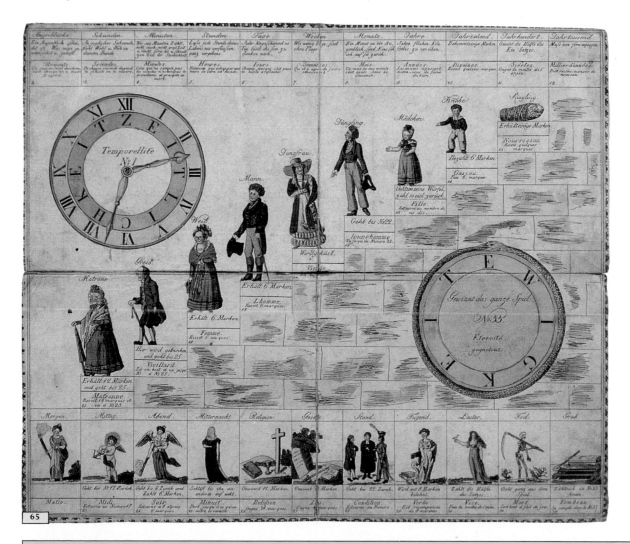

65

ELIZABETH NEWBERY, LONDON

Elizabeth Newbery was part of the Newbery family which were, during the 18th century, the leading publishers of literature for children.

Her establishment, from 1780 at the Corner of St Paul's Churchyard, was managed by John Harris who bought it in 1801. Many of her games and dissected puzzles were issued in conjunction with John Wallis, including The New Game of Human Life, *published in 1790.*

66

Veering away from the traditional race-game format and aimed rather more towards the teaching of behaviour and morals is *The Mount of Knowledge*, a hand-coloured engraving published in about 1800 by three different people working together – W Richardson of Greenwich, John Harris and John Wallis. The game takes the form of a path that wanders through a landscape dotted with small circular pictures showing woods and streams. The first circle, called the Horn Book, reflects one of the methods of teaching used at the time, and the accompanying instructions require the player to miss a turn to learn the letters of the alphabet or to 'give up all hope of gaining the Mount of Knowledge'. Circle 5, the Birch Wood, refers to flogging as a punishment, and if the player lands here, a forfeit may be paid to avoid the flogging. At circle 9, which represents Carelessness, however, the player is returned to Circle 5, and the punishment is meted out. Other punishments are given for straying, boasting, wasting time, idleness, self-indolence, obstinacy, ignorance, pride, conceit and forgetfulness, while the Rose, circle 16, is designed to teach that pleasure is sometimes attended with pain. The Primrose, on the other hand, asks the player to try to imitate its sweetness and simplicity. Most of the penalties fall within the first two-thirds of the game, so that by circle 44, the player has learnt all the harsh lessons and rewards may be given for recollection, repentance, patience, exertion and diligence. There are only 60 circles to contend with in this game, but many forfeits are imposed, requiring players to move backwards and to miss turns.

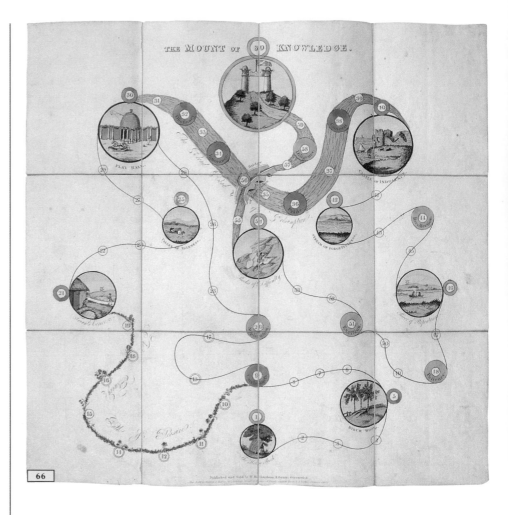

66

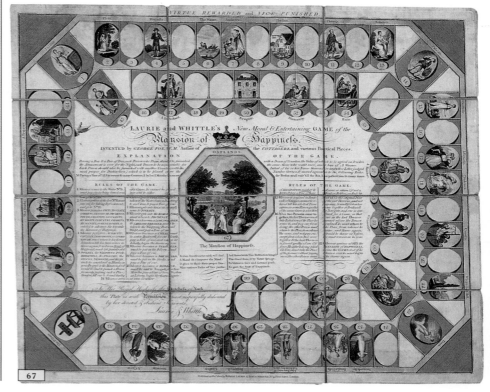

67

67

While most early board games bear the names of the publishers and the date of publication, few attest to the actual inventor if, of course, there was one. However, within the space of about one year, two moral games were 'invented' by one man, George Fox, although the publishers of the games differ. The first game, *The Mansion of Happiness,* is a hand-coloured engraving published by Robert Laurie and James Whittle on October 13th, 1800. It has 67 compartments, which represent various virtues and vices together with, in the centre (67), a view of Oatlands Park, the residence of the Duke of York. This game is very harsh compared with the others. The 'crimes' are serious – theft, lying, drunkenness, cheating – and the punishments include prison sentences, whipping, the stocks, and ducking. 'Whoever gets into a Passion must be taken to the Water, have a ducking to cool him and pay a fine of one.' *The Mansion of Happiness* is also the title of what is considered to be the first American board game, which was published by W & S B Ives in 1843 (see page 119).

68

A New, Moral and Entertaining Game of the Reward of Merit is comparatively lenient, and it uses animals and birds to illustrate many of the 37 compartments. Each illustration has a title and two lines of descriptive text, which includes any rewards or forfeits. As with most of these games, being good is rather boring compared with being naughty and the ratio is always about two forfeits to one reward. *The Reward of Merit,* a hand-coloured engraving, was published by John Harris and John Wallis on December 10th, 1801.

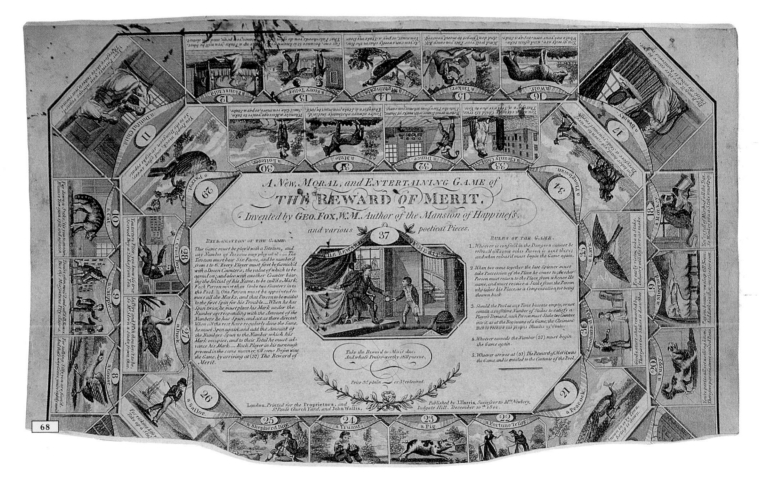

68

69

The New Game of Emulation is a hand-coloured engraving, published by John Harris on December 20th, 1804. It contains many allegories relating to the world a child may come in contact with – a shepherd tending his flock, a school, a church and a bishop, and even a rocking horse. All the 66 emblematic figures are designed to teach children to 'cheerfully exert themselves to obtain an honorary prize' while being 'perfectly aware of the consequences of disgrace and naturally dread it.'

70

Another game which uses scenes from everyday life to illustrate morals is *Every Man to His Station*. This hand-coloured engraving was published by Edward Wallis in about 1825.

71

Perhaps more interesting, now, than the game itself is the central illustration. It shows a group of boys actually playing the game *Every Man to His Station,* and using a teetotum which was considered more suitable than dice.

72

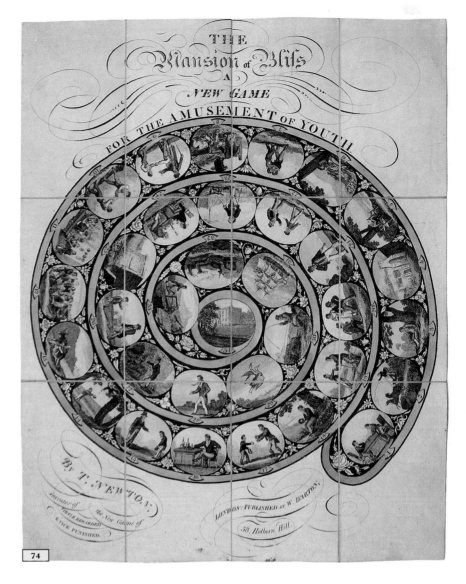

74

72

By the middle of the 19th century, the number of games of morals being published was decreasing as their methods of teaching became outdated. A very picturesque game was a lithograph published by William Spooner on November 1st, 1848, however, and this incorporated within its landscape a railway with the humorous title *Rattle Away Road*, rather suggesting what was thought of this new mode of transport. The game is played with a four-sided teetotum marked only for moves forwards, backwards, to the left and to the right, and the players followed the directions given. The full title of the game is *The Cottage of Content*, or *Right Road and Wrong Ways*. Each road has a meaningful title – Laughing Stock Lane, for example, where several boys are laughing at a man in the stocks – and the rewards and forfeits are marked on labels beside the roads – in this example 'Pay 2 for laughing'.

73

Two other games of which the inventor, Thomas Newton, is known, were published in 1818 and 1822 by William Darton. The earlier of the two bears the famous title *Virtue Rewarded and Vice Punished*. It has 33 medallions representing good and bad human characteristics and the game was designed for the amusement of youth 'with a view to promote the progressive improvement of the juvenile mind and to deter them from pursuing the dangerous paths of vice.'

73

74

The second game invented by Thomas Newton and published by William Darton, in 1822, is *The Mansion of Bliss*. It is also a hand-coloured etching in 12 sections mounted on linen. This game illustrates good and bad human characteristics by such references to the world around the players as Bridewell Prison, which was also used in George Fox's *Mansion of Happiness*. Interestingly, the rules for *The Mansion of Bliss* are written in four-line verse. Like *Virtue Rewarded and Vice Punished*, *The Mansion of Bliss* was designed for the amusement of youth 'with a view to promote the progressive improvement of the juvenile mind and to deter them from pursuing the dangerous paths of vice.'

75

William Spooner was also the publisher of a very similar game, which bore the title *The Journey* or *Cross Roads to the Conqueror's Castle.* Using humorous road titles and the same format of play as *The Cottage of Content,* the game is less moral but poses difficulties that must be overcome. For example, before attempting to pass along Mad Bull Lane, the player is told to 'take 2 from the Pool to raise your courage'. The Journey is a hand-coloured lithograph which was published by William Spooner between 1837 and 1846. The example illustrated is a reissue of the game; the original imprint was prior to 1836.

76

Considered by this author to be the least exciting game of its type ever produced, in which penalties are given for being good as well as for being bad, is *Willy's Walk to See Grandmamma,* published by A N Myers in 1869 as a hand-coloured lithograph. This spiral race game has no illustrations, and the rules and directions are written on the playing surface itself. There is no pool, and all rewards are made and forfeits paid by moving spaces or missing turns. Six compartments refer to Willy's accepting rides, hitherto regarded as a bad characteristic, but here they lead to advancement, while offering a poor child an apple or saving a dog from being teased leads to the penalty of missed turns.

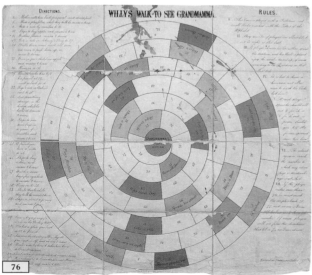

SNAKES AND LADDERS AND LUDO

Like other race games, *Snakes and Ladders* is a popular family game that relies on chance, in this case the throw of dice. When it was originally devised *Snakes and Ladders* was a moral game with virtues in the shape of the ladders, allowing the players to reach heaven quickly, while the vices, in the shape of snakes, forced the player back down. *Moksha-Patamu*, a similar game of Indian origin that was used for religious instruction, has 12 vices but only four virtues. Standard boards, showing just ladders and snakes, appeared as both squares and spirals – a spiral board was patented by A N Ayers in 1892, but some publishers retained the moral significance of the game.

77

The box of, *Willy's Walk to See Grandmamma* houses the game, the earthenware markers and a bone teetotum.

78

This version of *Snakes and Ladders* was printed in the 1950s by J & L Randall Ltd under the tradename Merit Games.

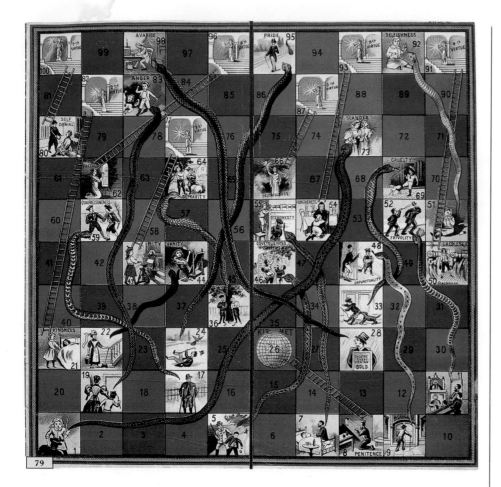

79

Kismet, the word meaning fate or destiny – stressed good and bad, and the game was intended to show a child that by being good and obedient, life would be more rewarding and generally more pleasant. Published as part of the Globe Series of Games and printed in Bavaria in about 1895, it has 100 squares, some of which are illustrated, 13 snakes and eight ladders.

81

Another example of *Snakes and Ladders* which was designed for the English market and printed in Bavaria in about 1895 ends with a scroll of names of well-known personalities whom the players would be expected to look up to as examples of hard-working or virtuous people.

80

The label pasted to the front of the *Kismet* board is very decorative. It is interesting to note here than women are presumed more virtuous than the unfortunate male.

82

The *Snakes and Ladders* format is used as the base of a 1920s English-produced game featuring the famous Tramp character portrayed by Charlie Chaplin. In this game, however, the ladder represents a downward slide instead of the normal upward climb. The yellow squares, containing stars and arrows, are the 'action' squares, indicating where the players must move.

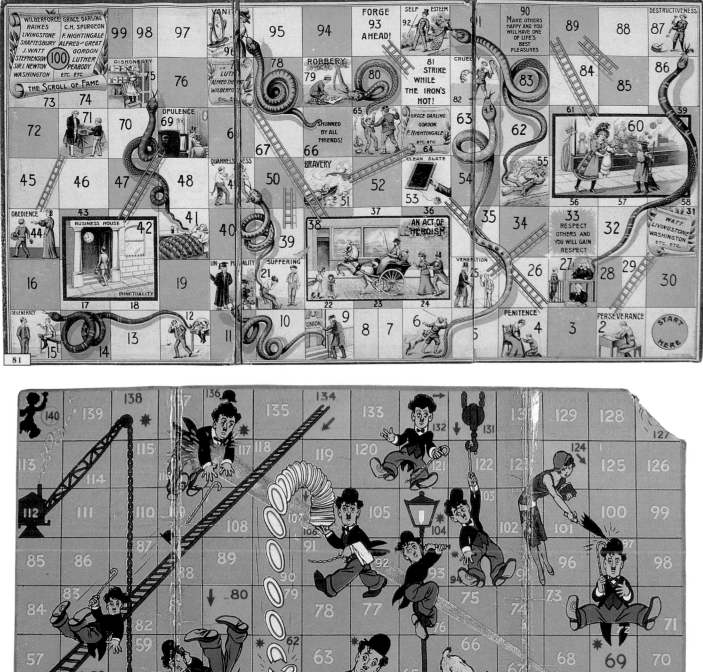

83

Literally taking climbing and sliding to their limit is the game *The Greasy Pole*, published in England at the beginning of the 20th century. Both the throw of the dice and the board directions determine whether a player moves up or down. Throwing a 3 allows a player to move up, whereas throwing 1 or 2 means that he or she moves down; red and yellow spots on the board are up moves, a brown spot means stay-where-you-are as 'you are out of breath', and a green spot indicates a fall to the ground.

84

The label on the box for the game *The Greasy Pole* illustrates the fact that this version of *Snakes and Ladders* was meant to amuse rather than moralize.

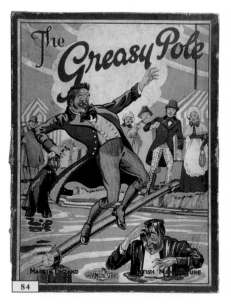

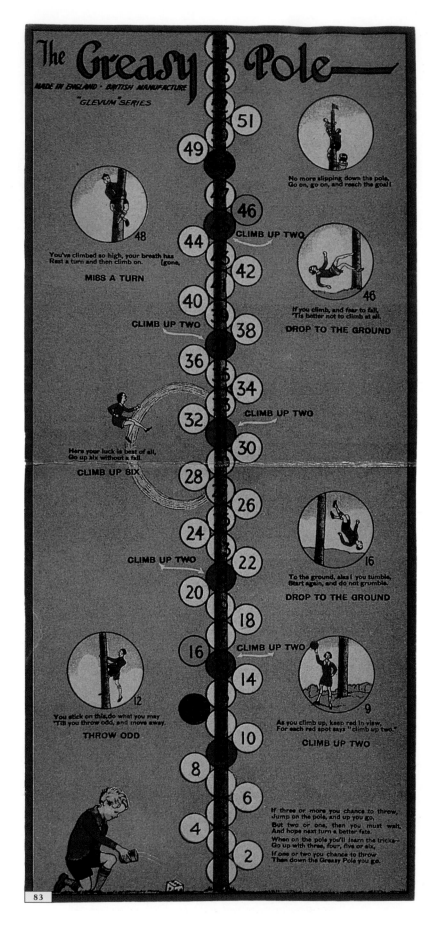

PACHISI AND LUDO

The other popular race game is *Ludo*. It is often one of the first games that young children learn to play as it requires no reading skills and can easily be taught and understood. The game is a derivation of *Pachisi*, the national game of India, and it was introduced into England towards the end of the 19th century.

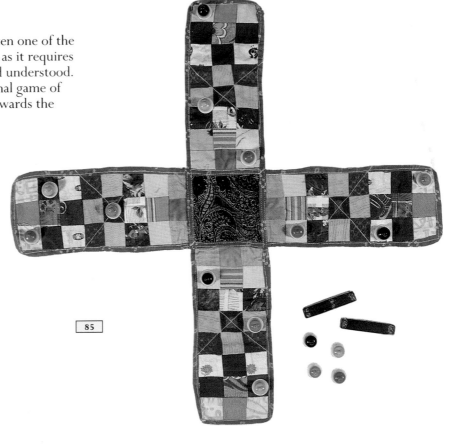

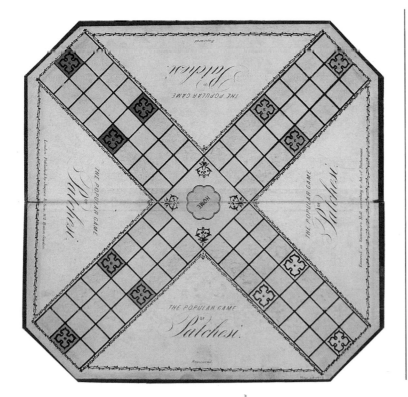

85

Pachisi is usually played on a cross-shaped panel of cloth created from a patchwork of different coloured and printed cottons. Expensive sets may have rock crystal markers, but usually the markers are made of wood. The game is often played with two large oblong dice, but equally six cowrie shells could be used, the number of moves being determined by the number of shells showing their openings uppermost. The aim is for a player to move all four of his or her markers around the board from start to finish. Markers may be captured and returned to the start, but 12 safe resting places, indicated by white stitching or other marks across the squares, are provided where this cannot happen. This version of *Pachisi* was made in India during the 1970s and is played on a patchwork of cotton with wooden markers and dice.

85

86

Ludo has the same aim as Pachisi but there are no resting places. European boards were designed in a number of different ways. Some had crosses set against diamond shapes, while some had crosses set against squares. The most common design and the one that is still in use is a cross with squares in each corner. *The Popular Game of Patchesi* [sic] was published by John Jaques & Sons Ltd. The company registered the tradename Patchesi in 1887 and used the same cross shape, set upon a diamond-shaped board.

86

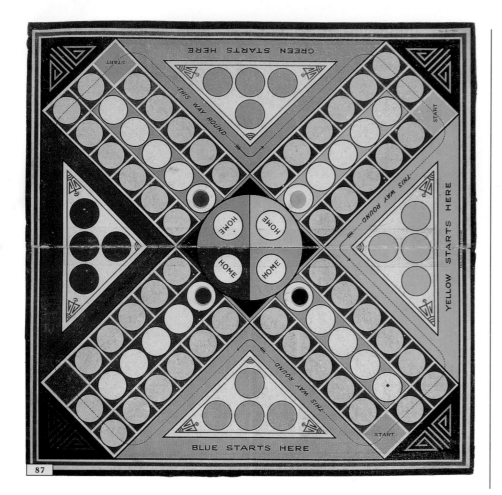

87

87

87

Ludo, The Ever Lasting Popular Game was published by the Chad Valley Company of Birmingham in the 1920s. This board shows a cross-shaped game set on a square.

88

This edition of *Ludo* was published by Berwick Toys in the 1950s. The board shows the shape that is widely accepted today of a cross with squares in each corner.

89

The version of *Ludo* that was published by Galt Toys in 1983 and designed by Barbara Sampson has a board that retains the cross and squares layout but also includes some rather fanciful cherry, orange, apple and lemon trees.

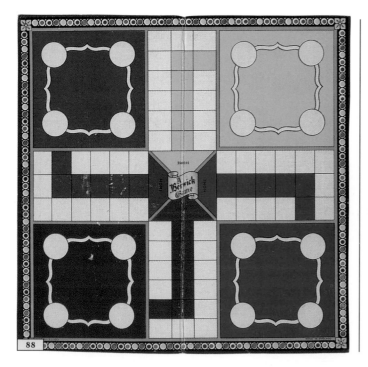

88

89

90

Several variations on basic *Ludo* have appeared. *Skudo* is a tactical *Ludo* game that was developed in the 1960s and published by John Waddington Ltd. The board is similarly marked out with the cross and squares layout, but four movable circles are added at the corners. If a marker lands on the Skudo square the player is allowed to turn the circle so that the marker may pass, and this shortens the player's route around the board.

91

John Waddington Ltd also published the game *Sorry* towards the end of the 1920s. It appeared in the 1934 Parker Brothers catalogue, classified as the 'most fashionable and largest selling game in England'. The aim is the same as in *Ludo* – that is to move four counters around the board to reach Home – but in *Sorry* the moves are governed by the draw of a card rather than the throw of dice. This particular example dates from the 1930s.

92

Tracks was produced by Galt Toys in 1983. The game is played much as *Ludo,* but the players have to collect the tracks made in the snow by people and animals.

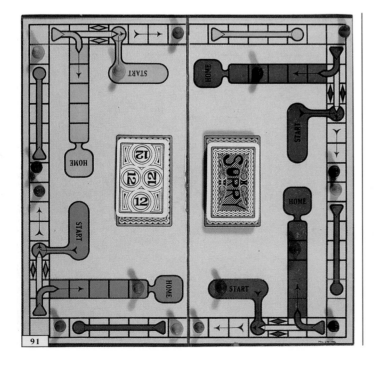

91

92

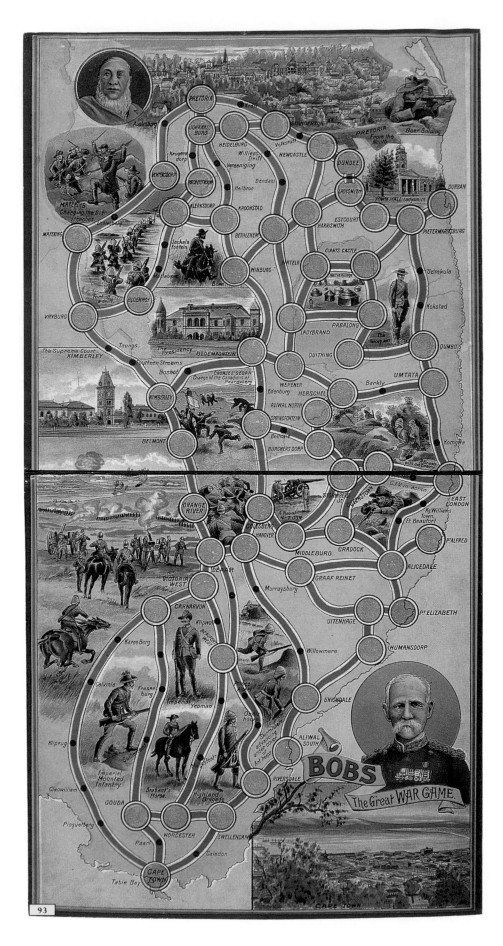

93

STRATEGY GAMES

Games for two people, in which they pit their wits or intellect against each other, are often referred to as strategy games. Within this overall name, however, are several quite different types – War Games, which generally include chess; Hunting Games, including *Fox and Geese* and *Halma*; and Alignment Games, such as *Nine Men's Morris*. All these games could be played by men, women and children, although some are now specially designed for one group or another. Some games were adapted for family use so that more than two people could play, although the structure and method of play retained the element of strategy.

94

93

Bob's Great War Game, published at the beginning of the 20th century (see page 74).

94

Chess, of course, may be played by anyone and it is probably the best-known game in the world. *Chess* boards have been made in many sizes, including ones for dolls' houses, and these days there are also computer based ones. This Chess set is based on the characters from Lewis Carroll's book, *Through the Looking Glass.* This colourful board is adorned with men of carved and painted wood representing the characters from the book. The whole game was designed and made by Robin and Nell Dale in 1983.

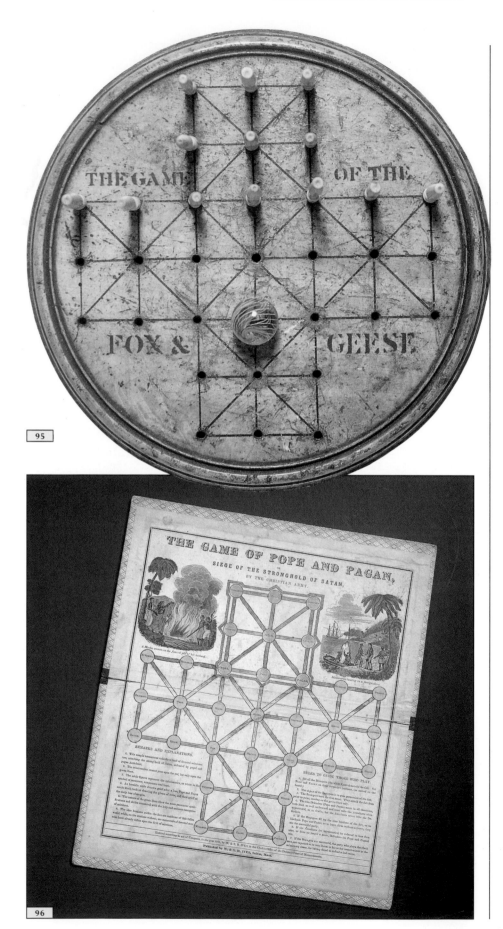

95

96

HUNTING GAMES

95

Fox and Geese is a hunting game with ill-matched forces; one player with one marker attempts to capture a multitude of his opponent's markers, while the opponent attempts to evade capture, and to surround the single marker and immobilize it. The moves each player is allowed to make govern the game. This example of *The Game of Fox and Geese* was played on a marked wooden board with bone geese and a glass marble fox. It was made in England in about 1850.

96

In America the game of Fox and Geese was also being published as a game of religious struggles. *The Game of Pope and Pagan* or *Siege of the Stronghold of Satan by the Christian Army* and its companion game *Mahomet and Saladin* or *The Battle for Palestine* were both published by W & S B Ives of Salem, Massachusetts. The game shows hand coloured illustrations in the upper corners and the rules of play in the lower corners. The publishing details are along the bottom and read: Entered according to the Art of Congress in the year 1844 by W & S B Ives in the Clerk's Office of the District Court of Massachusetts. *Mahomet and Saladin* was published two years later in 1846.

97

Halma, which was issued in 1888 by A N Ayers and published by a number of different companies for many years, requires the players to move all their markers from one corner of a board with 256 squares to the opposing corner from which their opponent started. More than two players, usually working in pairs, can play the game of *Halma,* and it is also possible to play it as a game of *Solitaire.* This example of the game was published by John Jaques & Sons Ltd in about 1900.

98

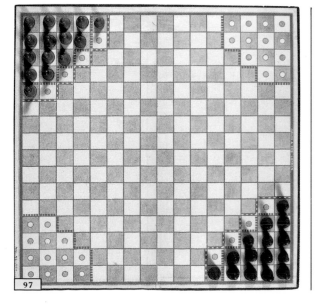

97

98

Also first published in 1888 was *Chivalry, The Popular Game of Skill*. Copyrighted by Geo. S Parker & Co. the game is more like Draughts as opponent's men may be removed from the board when they are captured.

99

An adaptation of the game *Halma* is *Chinese Checkers*. In both games the markers remain on the board, and the winner is the player who not only reaches his or her corner first but gets all his or her markers into the corner. This painted metal board with marbles for playing *Chinese Checkers* was made in the United States in the 1950s.

99

100

A second example of a *Chinese Checkers* game, which was made in England in 1977 by Just Games Trading Co, has a polished wooden board and glass marbles.

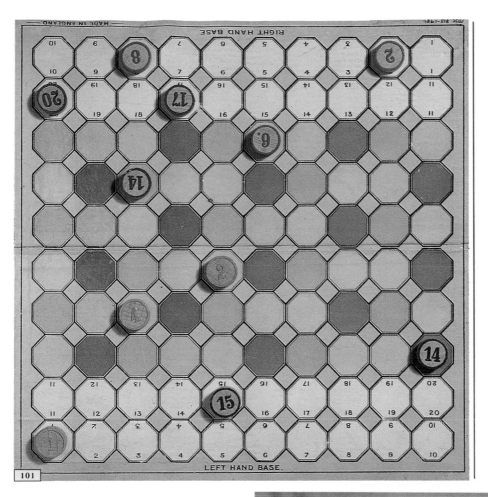

101

The New Game of Colorito was published by Hayford & Sons in the 1920s. A variation on *Halma*, the game has two sets of 20 numbered markers. The aim of the game is to move these from one end of the board to the other and into appropriately numbered squares. All the markers remain on the board but must be on a square of a corresponding colour.

101

102

A modern game, which is somewhat of a cross between a Hunt Game and an Alignment Game is *Caesar's Game*, which was devised by Michael Kindred and Malcom Goldsmith for Waddingtons Games Ltd in 1984. It is played with gold and silver columns, representing the building of empires, and coins, representing wealth, on a board marked with similarly coloured circles and diamonds. The aim is to move the columns of one colour into a square shape anywhere in the central part of the board. However, moves may be attempted only if there is a coin of either colour on a diamond adjacent to the column and a vacant circle of the same colour. The coins may also be moved to help or hinder the players, and 'traps' may be arranged by using the coins to block a column, which must then be removed to the perimeter starting point.

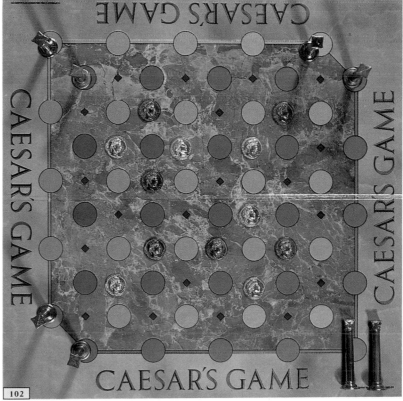

102

GAMES OF ALIGNMENT

103

Peg'ity, Spoil Five and *Quintro* are three games of alignment that were produced in the 1920s. They are almost identical, the aim being to achieve a straight line of pegs, while preventing opponents from doing the same. A grid of holes and a group of wooden pegs are provided, and the games may be played with up to four players. In these cases, the boxes are more inviting to look at than those of the games boards, and two show people playing the game. *Peg'ity,* made of cardboard and wood, was produced in the United States by Parker Brothers.

104

Various wars of the 19th century in which the United States took part, including the Civil War, have been the bases for a number of games. One, simply called *Game of Strategy,* was copyrighted in 1891 by McLoughlin Brothers. It has a coloured lithographed playing board which shows a cavalry headquarters in the centre and the implements of war in each corner. There are 16 black and 16 white counters and a spinner with two arrows. Spinners are very much an American games features at a time when dice or teetotum were being used in English and European games. It must be remembered that the three major producers of games were located in the north east, either New England or New York. The Civil War had a great impact on the country and most of the games reflected a win by the northern troops which included the US Cavalry.

103

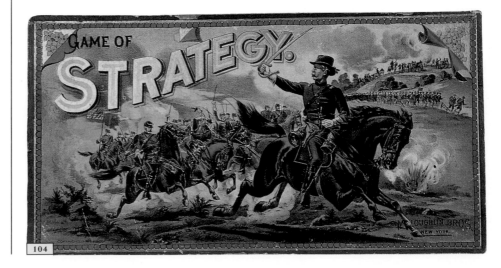

104

105

Spoil Five, also made of cardboard and wood, was produced by the Chad Valley Company of Birmingham.

105

PARKER BROTHERS, SALEM, MASSACHUSETTS

The company was established by George S Parker when he acquired the rights to W & S B Ives in 1887. It is still a major publisher of games and other toys, though in the last 20 years has had a rather checkered history: the company, along with other American and British publishers such as Chad Valley, became part of the General Mills Fun Group which was sold off from 1985 onwards. It is now part of Kenner Parker Tonka. During its independent life the company introduced many novel and original games, based on the American way of life, sports and hobbies as well as financial pursuits, as made popular in the games of Pit *and* Monopoly.

106

106

Quintro was produced by Spears of Enfield, North London. Like *Peg'ity* and *Spoil Five,* it is made of cardboard and wood.

107

Checklines is a plastic board game manufactured by Tri-Ang in about 1970. It is a game for two players, each of whom has five men in the form of lions and unicorns. The aim is to complete two straight lines using the five men while impeding your opponent.

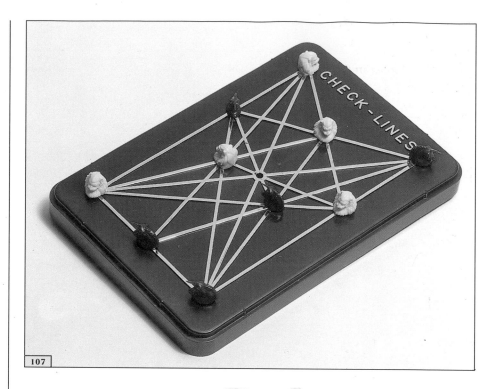

107

108

Recently, especially since the advent of plastic, three dimensional strategy games based on *Noughts and Crosses* have been introduced. These task the players' abilities to see and understand problems arising from having to move markers in several different directions at one time. *Spacelines, The 3-D Puzzle of the Future* was produced in the 1980s by Invicta Plastics and is basically a game of *Noughts and Crosses*.

108

STRATEGY GAMES AND WAR

The armed forces and war have inspired a number of games, perhaps following the late 18th century tradition of celebrating the exploits of king and country in board games. Strategy games were naturally the easiest to transform into battle games of all types. Men at war, be they soldiers, seamen or pilots, would play games in their spare time, often creating their own simple boards from paper and pencil, and re-enacting famous victories.

109

The Game of Besieging was published in Germany between 1800 and 1820. It uses the *Fox and Geese* format with shaped wooden men.

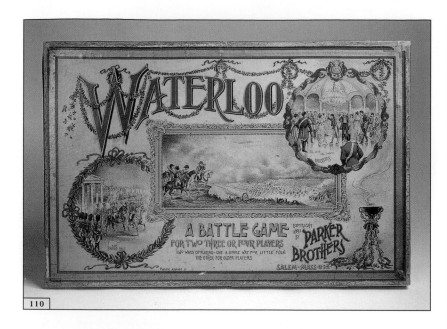

110

111

Although the United States was not involved in the Battle of Waterloo, the rise and fall of Napoleon I did lead to some fascinating games. Nearly a century after the event Parker Brothers copyrighted in 1985 a game simply called *Waterloo, a Battle Game for Two, Three or Four Players*. The box label shows three scenes, Napoleon in Paris in 1815 and a dance in Brussels with the centre devoted to the battle itself being watched by Napoleon. The board itself is criss crossed with red lines and white dots and has in each corner the representation of a town (Paris, Versaille, Brussels and Ligny Namur) with the towns of Quatre Bras and Charlesroi in the central area. The game may be played in a simple way for young children or in a second, more complicated way for older children and adults. It is similar to the Boar War game *Bobs*.

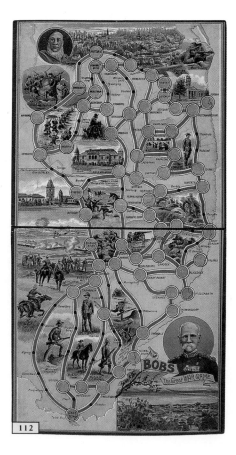

112

111

A New Game of Russia v Turkey, a hand-coloured lithograph, was published by J A Reeves in about 1853.

112

Conflicts at the end of the 19th century produced several national heroes, of whom Lord Kitchener and Lord Roberts were among the most famous. Games based on their exploits soon appeared. *Bobs, The Great War Game*, deals with the Boer War; it is a game of strategy in which both players attempt to reach their goals while halting the progress of their opponent. This game was part of the Globe Series of Games, published between 1900 and 1910.

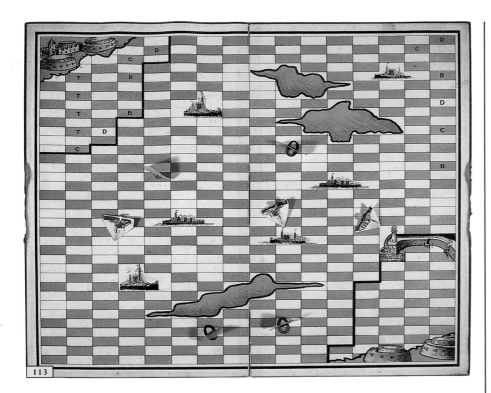

113

113

Halma may also be seen as the root of many such games. Published by Mead & Field Ltd of London shortly before the outbreak of the First World War, *Transports*, requires the red side to move its transports from one safe harbour to another while under the protection of battleships, destroyers and cruisers. Its enemy, the Black Fleet, attempts to capture the red side's transports. Rules govern the movement of each vessel, and there are a number of 'islands' that have to be avoided, while the Black Fleet is not allowed to enter the harbours. The game is won or lost if the transports are successful.

114

Sink The Submarine, also published around the First World War, is a straightforward race game with all the directions of play written on the illustrated squares. This game is without maker's name or marking and therefore the publisher remains unknown.

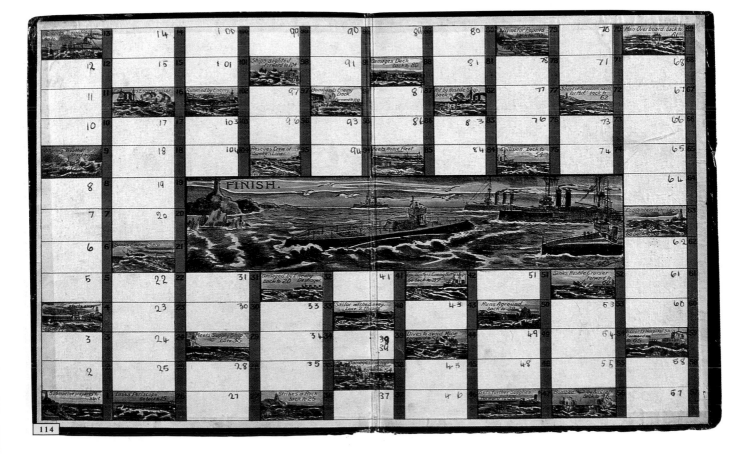

114

115

116

115

After the war, H P Gibson & Sons Ltd issued four games of strategy, three of which are Halma types. *L'attaque, The Famous Game of Military Tactics* was devised in France and features British and French forces. This example shows the playing surface.

116

Dover Patrol or *Naval Tactics* requires the capture of the enemy's flag. Shown here is the lid of the box; the playing surface is similar to that of *L'Attaque*.

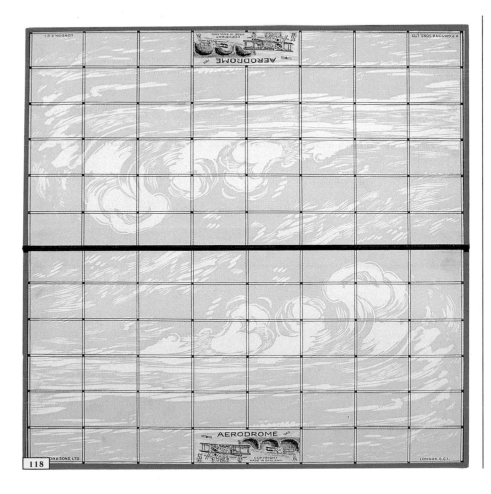

117

Aviation is an aerial tactics game of attack and defence. This example is the lid of the box .

118

The fourth game which was published by H P Gibson & Sons Ltd, *The New Game of Jutland*, was played rather like noughts and crosses but the opponents cannot see each other's moves. All four games continued to be reissued for many years.

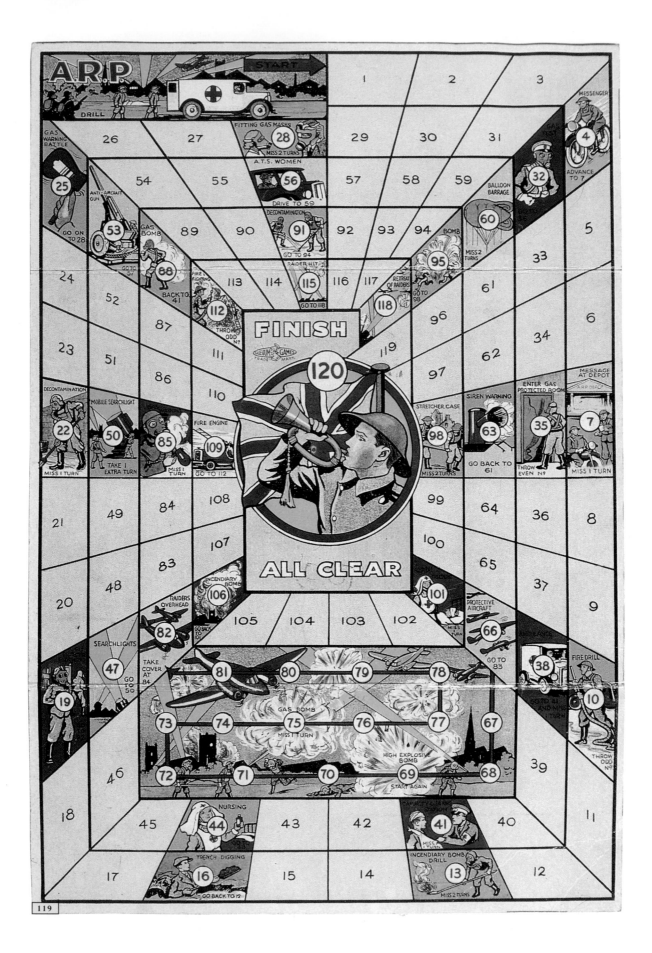

The Second World War generated a number of games, some of which were meant to be fun while others had educational leanings. *A.R.P.* is played as a normal race game with rewards and forfeits. The game illustrates many of the jobs done and the dangers encountered during the war years, and it was inspired by the air raid precautions – *A.R.P.* – necessary at the time.

120

Another race game, arising from the Second World War and said, on its instructions, to be like *Snakes and Ladders*, is the light-hearted *Annie Wants Her Stripes*. More recent conflicts, while represented in other forms of toys, have not been portrayed as games.

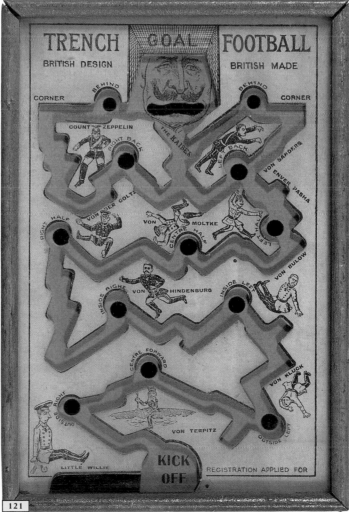

121

Not all games featuring war are board games; card and dexterity games have been based on martial themes as well. *Trench Football*, which has the impressive sub-title 'The Great International Game by the Makers of the sensationally Successful War Game *The Silver Bullet*', takes the form of a wooden box with a glass top. The playing surface is covered with a series of cut out grooves along which at intervals appear holes, named after German commanders. The aim is to move a metal ball along the grooves without it dropping down a hole.

122

England Expects, the Great Naval Card Game was published in the 1940s as a set of 44 cards. The game was devised with the help of Francis E McMurtrie, who was, at the time, editor of *Jane's Fighting Ships.*

GAMES AND SPORTS

Sporting activities have inspired many games, especially in the 20th century, although most of these games follow the formats already laid down by earlier games. Horse racing and, in particular, steeplechasing, however, gave rise to a new design of board. This board, which is often folded in two places rather than the conventional one, is longer, the playing surface is lozenge-shaped and has narrow, angled compartments. Although the compartments tend to be rather sparsely decorated, the boards themselves are lavishly illustrated with racing scenes, the onlookers, and the start and finish of the race. The actual rules of the game are still based on forfeits and rewards, with turns missed and players moving forwards and backwards as directed.

125

This example of *Steeple-Chase* is a hand-coloured lithograph published by Watilliaux of Paris in about 1860. The compartments are numbered from 1 to 100 and the game has five fences, with a fallen rider and horse at the second. The central illustration and those around the edge of the board depict the thrills and spills associated with the race.

123

Two games that may perhaps be regarded as bridging the gap between military-based games and normal games are devoted to the Scouting movement. One is a strategy game, the other a race game, but both were issued by Chad Valley as part of a *Boy's Own* compendium, which also included *Snakes and Ladders*, races around the world and across Canada, and a number of table games such as *Blow Football*. *Scouting* is a *Fox and Geese* game for between two and six players. The aim is for one player (the dispatch runner) to take papers from the field officer at the top of the board to the camp at the bottom and then to return without being captured or hemmed in by the patrol of Scouts, which has been sent out to intercept the message.

124

Scouting Tests is a straightforward race game, which starts at Enrolment and moves to the right. Accompanying the game are test cards and badges, which determine the rewards and forfeits, and these must be paid out for surprise tests and the commissioners' inspection. The winner is the one who reaches presentation of the Silver Wolf badge, which is just to the left of enrolment.

125

81

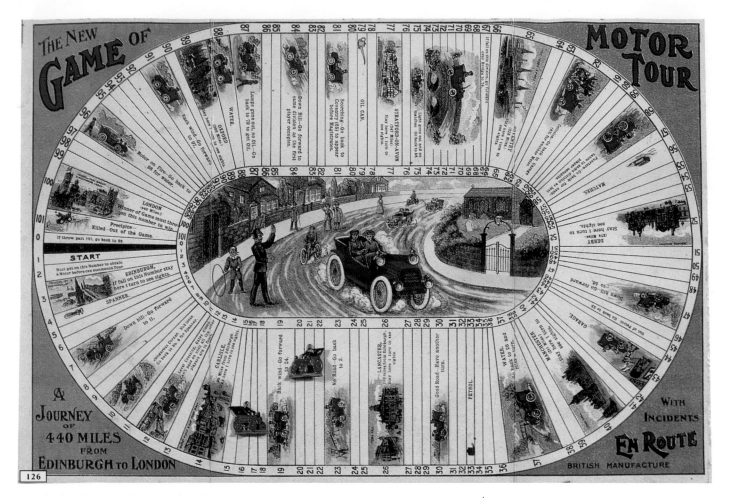

127

126

The steeplechase format, while continuing to illustrate horse racing, was adapted to show other types of racing – cars, greyhounds and even motorcycles. Sometimes the boards are highly decorated, sometimes not, but each attempts to show the perils of what are often quite dangerous sports. In *The New Game of Motor Tour*, the board is numbered from 1 (the Start) to 100 (London) with 101 and 0 after 100. The winner is the player who lands on 100; if a player lands on 101, he must leave the game as he is deemed to have fallen over a precipice and been killed. If a throw takes players to 0 or beyond, they must return to compartment 86. The game was probably published by The Chad Valley Company of Birmingham in about 1912.

127

Shown here is the box lid of *The New Game of Motor Tour*, subtitled 'From Edinburgh to London, a Journey of 440 Miles with Thrilling Incidents *en Route*.'

128

The game of *Motor Cycle Racing* attempts to show all the thrills and spills of this rather noisy sport while remaining a rather sedate indoor board game. It was published as part of a compendium of games and is designed for four players. The centre of the circuit shows a vivid, modern illustration of a motorcycle race in progress.

129

Although it looks very similar, *Greyhound Racing* is, in fact, played in a slightly different manner as the hare must be advanced on its own track at the same time as the dogs. This is achieved by using two dice, of different sizes: the smaller one determines the movement of the hare, the larger one that of the dogs. The dogs are moved by the players individually when their turn comes round, but the hare is moved at each throw of the dice. To win, a dog can either land in the same compartment as the hare or pass the winning post, but the dogs may not pass the hare, and those that might, lose a turn. Losing a turn is also the penalty if a dog lands in a compartment already occupied as 'it is supposed a fight ensues'. The game, which was published in the Glevum Series in the 1930s, has lead dogs and hare, made by Britains Ltd.

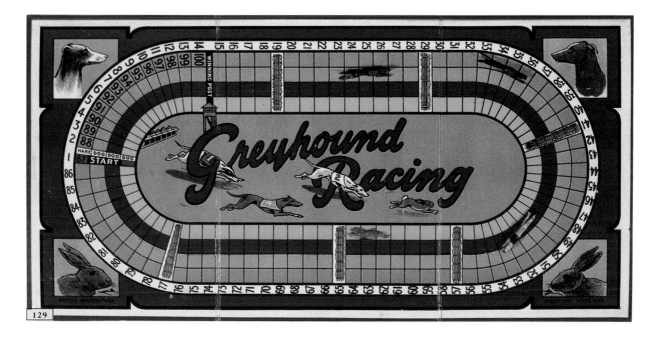

130

130

Soccer has been the inspiration of several games, as have American football, golf and cricket. Some of these are devised to be played just for fun, while others are designed to help with skills such as manual dexterity and arithmetic. *Soccatelle* is a bagatelle game made of wood. There are two pull springs at the bottom, one representing the shooter and the other the goalkeeper. The game was published by Chad Valley in the 1920s.

131

Goal, The Soccer Card Game was published about 1965 as a set of 44. The cards are referred to as 'action cards' because the illustrations show British teams, their emblems and the positions of play used in a game of soccer.

131

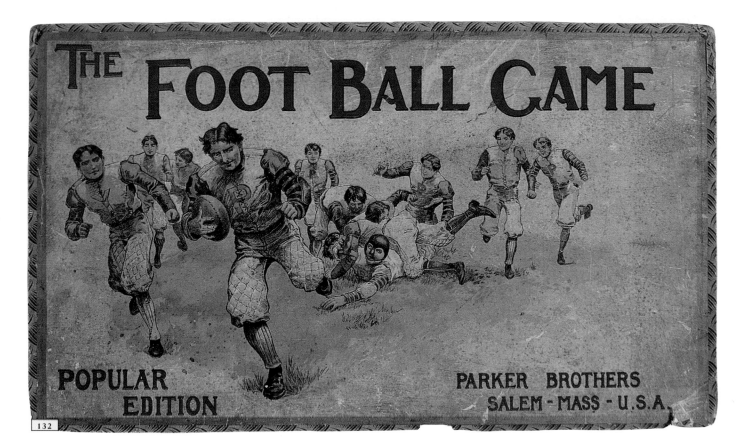

132

132

The Foot Ball Game was published by Parker Brothers of Salem, Massachusetts, in about 1910. The box is shown here. With the game is a cardboard spinner marked with two circles. The outer circle directs the moves to be played, and the inner one the numbers of yards the football may be advanced.

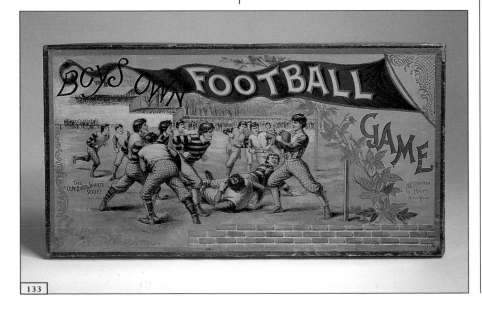

133

McLoughlin Brothers also published a game based on football with the title *Boy's Own Football Game*. Produced in 1901, the game is part of the Great Outdoor Sports Series. As seen with other American publishers of the time, McLoughlin Brothers used the trick of having the playing surface on the inside of the bottom of the box, thus reducing the cost of the game as a third piece of card was not necessary and the box became both storage for the various pieces of equipment and the game itself.

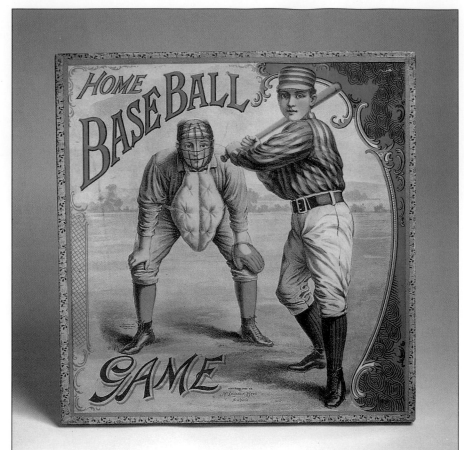

134

134

This method of production was also used by McLoughlin Brothers for the *Home Baseball Game* which was based on the ever popular American game. McLoughlin Brothers copyrighted the game in 1890.

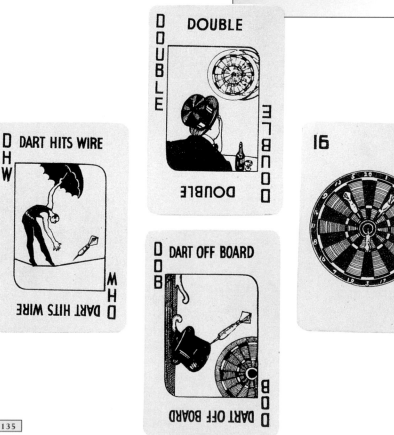

135

135

Popular games of the kind often played in public houses have also been adapted as children's games – darts and shove ha'penny being just two examples. Such games are not always shown in the same manner. *Dartex* is a card game which, judging from the rather sophisticated illustrations, may well have been devised for adults rather than children, although either could play. Certainly children would brush up their adding and subtracting skills by playing this game. *Dartex, The Thrilling New Card Game of Skill* was published by R L Smith of Cranleigh, Surrey in 1938. Of the cards, 38 show a dart board and a score, while 15 show illustrations and directions.

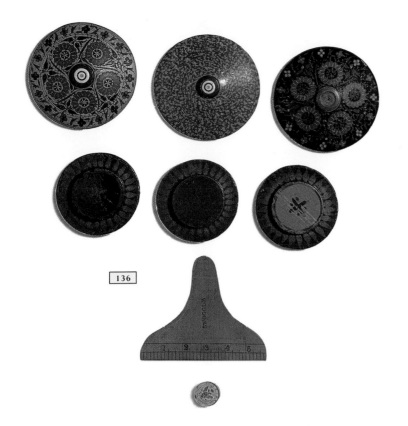

136

Squails, which is played on a smooth table top, is a combination of shove ha'penny and bowls. First, a jack is flicked along a smooth surface, and then the discs are flicked. Those discs of one player that are the closest to the jack win the game. Parts of two sets of *Squails* are shown here, both of which are of painted wood. Also shown is a measuring device called a 'swoggle'. The smaller discs were made in England by John Jaques & Sons Ltd after 1884; the larger set was made in India at about the same time.

137

Not all games with a sporting theme need to represent official games; some may show activities such as tobogganing in the snow that can be enjoyed by everyone. *The Game of Toboganning* was published by Chad Valley in the 1930s. The players can really enjoy all the fun and spills of playing in the snow.

137

Dolphin.

Vol. II. page 9

Pub. Oct 3. 1801 by J. Marshall N.º 4 Aldermary Church Yard

CARDS AND CARD GAMES

The origins of playing cards are surrounded in mystery. They are thought to have appeared in China during the Tang dynasty (AD 618–907), but it was not until the late 1300s that cards were first introduced in Europe.

Cards specifically designed for the amusement and education of children did not appear until the second half of the 1700s. Those produced at this time tended to have pictorial themes rather than the numerical, jack, queen and king form with which we are familiar today. These early sets of cards were produced, using the same methods of printing and colouring, by established publishers of other children's games, such as John Wallis.

Some of the surviving card games are well documented bearing the publisher's name, date of publication and all the directions of play, and are complete sets. Unfortunately, not all games are well documented or even complete, but even so, it is possible to decide, by their nature or design, which game could be played with a particular set of cards.

A huge variety of games has been devised over the years, the best known of which are in the *Happy Families* format. However, cards were also used to tell fairy tales, ask and answer questions on a wide range of subjects, illustrate nature, animals and places, and even to teach foreign languages.

Although not strictly card games, a few are linked with those mentioned because of their educational values. These include games like *Scrabble* and *Shake Spell*, and those that technically could be classified as card games but that, like *Lotto*, are also games of chance. *Scrabble, Shake Spell* and the earlier sets of *Alphabet* discs all have letters of the alphabet on small, round or square blocks. These letters are used to learn the alphabet itself and to create words from the letters. *Scrabble* and *Shake Spell* have the advantage over earlier sets as they incorporate multiples of the most frequently used letters. The alphabet sets were usually made of bone, and were often attractively decorated.

CARDS AND EDUCATION

A wide range of subjects was taught using cards. Not all the card sets formed games, many being simply single illustrations as with natural history subjects, although they were occasionally accompanied by a booklet describing each of the illustrations. Not all the pictures were true to life, as the artist may not have seen nor even read about the animal described.

138

The Infant's Cabinet of Fishes, a set of 27 cards accompanied by a booklet, was published using hand-coloured etchings by John Marshall on October 3rd, 1801. One illustration, that of a dolphin fish, looks a little crude by today's standards, but its accompanying description reads: 'The principle beauty of this fish is its colours which are very brilliant.'

139

The Good Child's Cabinet of Natural History, Embellished with 32 Fine Engravings, Volume 1: Beasts, on the other hand, includes the descriptive text on each card. Published by John Wallis on January 4th, 1813, the set of 32 cards is housed in a wooden box with a sliding lid decorated with a palm tree and antelope. Apart from describing the rhinoceros as a unicorn, the details given for some of the animals are also unusual and inaccurate. The zebra is said to 'surpass all others in swiftness', while of the wolf the card says: 'They were formerly very common in the country; but happily have long been extirpated.' The example shown here, the rhinoceros, is a hand-coloured engraving.

THE RHINOCEROS

Is nearly as large as the elephant; it is armed with a kind of horn on its nose, and its skin is so hard, as to resist a musket ball; it inhabits Africa, and is what is called the Unicorn in holy writ.

139

PEACOCK

140

140

Published in about 1850 was a game entitled *Grandmamma's New Game of Natural History*. It has two parts; the first is a game showing fairy tale characters and matching cards, while the second comprises 36 cards illustrating animals and birds together with descriptions and four-line verses. The example shown, the peacock, is a hand-coloured engraving.

EDUCATIONAL CARD GAMES

The card games played from the late 18th century until the introduction of *Happy Families* in about 1860, were governed by several different sets of rules, but most were games of forfeiture.

By far the simplest set of rules requires all the cards to be dealt and one player to be chosen as leader or president. He asks each player in turn a question; a correct answer is rewarded with a counter from the kitty, a wrong answer means the player must pay into the kitty. The questions are a test of general knowledge; for example, the geography questions want to know in what country or county a particular town, river or hill is, or what the principal product of a town is. On the whole, the cards are numbered on both sides and a game can be played in number rotation until one of the players has no cards left and wins. In this game, when a player gives a wrong answer, the next person to play begins with his or her lowest numbered card.

The majority of games played with these rules deal with historical or geographical subjects, but languages and grammar were also sometimes introduced. *The Geography of England and Wales, Accurately Delineated* was published by John Wallis on September 26, 1799 and printed by James Harrison of Warwick Court, London. The set consists of 52 numbered cards, each of which gives a county of England or Wales, its boundaries,

principal towns and products and general characteristics. A footnote to the rules reads: 'by which means the cards will be rendered not only instructive but amusing and entertaining.' This set shows the move from an agricultural to an industrial society and it was published at the beginning of the Industrial Revolution. The list of manufacturers combined with the descriptions of the countryside must have been a revelation to many.

Published five years later by John Harris, *A New and Compendious System of Geography on Cards* deals with countries of the world. The set has 56 cards, on which the details are given, and one card, on which the geographical terms employed are explained. Issued with the cards is an eight-page booklet describing the educational benefits of the cards and its final sentences sum up the approach of adults to teaching children in the early years of the 19th century:

> Experience, however, shews [sic] that children are soon capable of making a considerable Progress in this Science, which is principally an Object of Sense and Memory. Any judicious Person will consider it as a Matter of serious Importance to give them an early Acquaintance with Words and Things, and especially to initiate them in those Studies that tend to gratify their natural Curiosity, to open and enlarge the Mind, to promote a Spirit of Enquiry and inspire the Love of Knowledge.

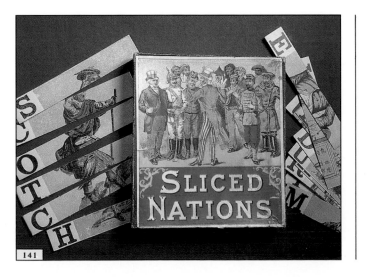

141

An American card game which linked spelling and geography was published about 1890 by Selchow & Righter of New York with the appropriate title *Sliced Nations*. The elongated cards each have a letter of the alphabet and part of an illustration. The aim is to collect all the cards for one nationality and make up a set. It may now be considered that the illustrations were not appropriate, in fact possibly even degrading, but at the time of publication this was not the intention and the game was classified as most suitable.

30

92. Name some of the eminent men who died in this reign.

92. *The Marquis of Londonderry, Lord Byron, the Duke of York, George Canning, and Sir Thomas Lawrence.*

93. What are the names of four fascinating poets whose works are so generally admired?

93. *Sir Walter Scott, Thomas Moore, Lord Byron, and Robert Southey.*

1831 to 1837.

94. William IV. ascended the throne on the death of his royal brother, Whom did he marry?

94. *Adelaide of Saxe-Meiningen, in 1818.*

95. The Queen of William IV. having survived him, what was her title?

95. *Queen Dowager.*

96. A very important Bill passed both houses of Parliament, and received the royal assent; What is the name of it?

96. *The Reform Bill.*

31

1837.

97. Victoria, on the death of her uncle, William IV., ascended the throne, What was her late father's title?

97. *Duke of Kent.*

98. At what age did Queen Victoria ascend the throne?

98. *In her nineteenth year.*

99. When was the Queen married?

99. *On the 10th of February, 1840.*

100. To whom was the Queen married?

100. *Her cousin, Prince Albert of Saxe-Coburg-Gotha.*

Stevens & Co., Printers, Bell Yard, Fleet Street.

VICTORIA. BRUNSWICK.

Began to reign 1837.
Born 1819.
Whom God preserve!

Duke of Kent.

In her nineteenth year.

On the 10th of February, 1840.

Her cousin, Prince Albert, of Saxe Coburg Gotha.

142

Games with kings and queens were always firm favourites, at least among adults. *Historical Amusements – A New Game*, was published by Nicholas Carpenter in 1844. It consists of a booklet, 36 cards showing medallion portraits of monarchs from William I to Queen Victoria and 100 small cards with printed answers. The game requires the players to collect the small cards that relate to the larger ones, and these are, in fact, the answers to questions posed in the booklet, although the booklet also showed the answers. *Queen Victoria* is the last set, with questions 97 to 100. The illustrated cards are hand-coloured engravings, while the small cards are printed by letterpress.

143

Some time after 1870, John Jaques published a group of three card games covering the reigns of English and British monarchs from William I to Queen Victoria. Each has the rather strange title *A Game of Hide and Seek With Kings and Queens of England*. The game is played in the same manner as *The Counties of England* (see page 98), with the players attempting to collect the additional cards that accompany the main picture card to create sets or tricks. The player with the most tricks wins. The cards relating to Henry VIII and Queen Anne were produced as hand-coloured lithographs and printed by letterpress. The main card names important events and people associated with the lives of the monarchs, and these are listed individually on the additional cards. Some groups are larger than others, with the largest consisting of a total of seven cards.

144

American presidents were similarly treated. *Game of Columbia's Presidents* was designed to teach the names and dates of each man. The cards bear an illustration of one man, his dates and signature and the names of others closely associated with him. President Grant, a general during the Civil War, is illustrated on the cover. McLoughlin Brothers published this card game in 1890.

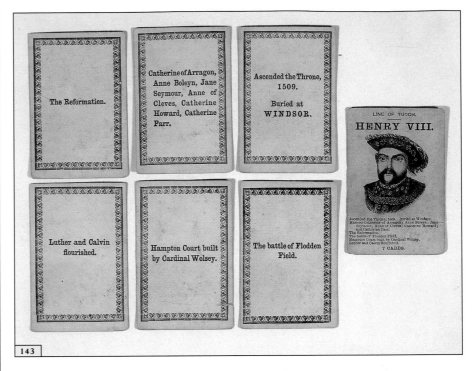

143

144

The teaching of languages, and not only English, was treated differently from the geographical and historical subjects. English grammar was inculcated by *Grammatical Conversations or English Grammar Familiarised,* in which the cards are divided into two sets, one with the questions and the other with the answers. The answer cards are dealt, while one person, probably an older child or adult, holds the questions and key card. As each question is asked and answered correctly, the players relinquish their cards. Whoever is first to get rid of his or her cards wins. A gambling element could be introduced by having a pool and rewards and forfeits.

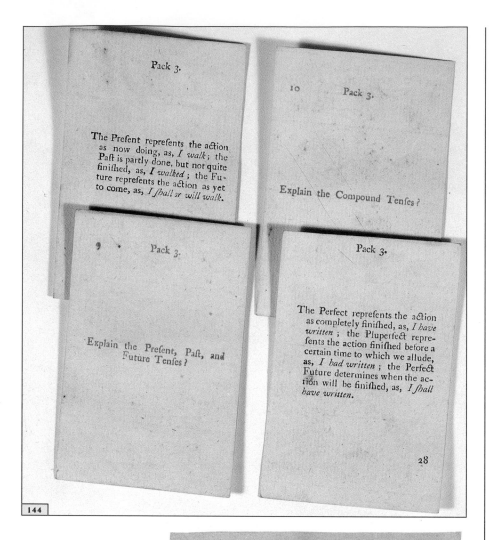

144

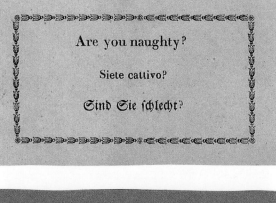

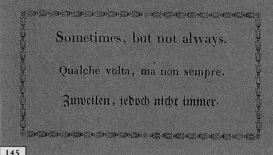

145

144

The teaching of languages, both foreign and native, was treated differently from the geographical and historical subjects. English grammar was inculcated by *Grammatical Conversations* or *English Grammar Familiarised*, in which the cards are divided into two sets, one with the questions and the other with the answers. The answer cards are dealt, while one person, probably an older child or adult, holds the questions and key card. As each question is asked and answered correctly, the players relinquish their cards. Whoever is first to get rid of his or her cards wins. A gambling element could be introduced by having a pool and rewards and forfeits. *Grammatical Conversations or English Grammar Familiarised* was printed by letterpress on card. The set consists of 60 cards and was produced in about 1790 by an unknown publisher.

145

A set of 32 cards arranged in a similar manner has questions and answers in four languages. Entitled *Le Petit Questionneur Polyglotte, Choix de Questions Enfantines, en Anglais, en Italien, en Allemand, et en Français*, the game was published by A La Libraire Française et Anglaise de Truchy, 18 Boulevard des Italiens, Paris, in about 1850. The French version is on one side of the cards, and the rest of the languages are on the other side. One card of the set, entitled 'Are You Naughty' was printed by letterpress on card. A footnote to the title *Le Petit Questionneur Polyglotte* reads: 'Exercises Propres à Exciter Les Enfants à La Conversation.' It seems likely that children could have found something more exciting to play.

This game and *Grammatical Conversations* were beginning to reflect the importance being given to the precepts of good behaviour, which were strongly reflected in contemporary board games such as *Virtue Rewarded and Vice Punished*.

146

The teaching of French with cards continued throughout the 19th and well into the 20th century. Using pictures was probably more satisfying for the players and, when combined with methods of play already learned, the process of learning a foreign language no doubt became easier. *Amusement for Beginners in French*, a hand-coloured engraving, was published by John Betts in about 1855. The set has 210 cards, showing pictures and titles, which have been cut in half. The top half has the English name and upper part of the picture, while the French name and its phonetic title are shown with the lower half of the picture. The game could be played by one person or in the same way as dominoes.

146

147

147

French for Fun, a New Instructive and Amusing Card Game was printed by chromolithography. John Jaques & Son of London published this game during the 1930s, and it contains 32 cards, each of which bears an illustration, a sentence and a list of the other cards needed to make up a set. It follows the rules Jaques set down for *The Counties of England.*

JOHN BETTS, LONDON

John Betts was one of the leading publishers of children's games and dissected puzzles during the 19th century. He did, in fact, produce a number of teaching aids other than these, including globes and table games. Between 1827 and 1845, his address is listed as 7 Compton Street, Brunswick Square, then as 115 The Strand until 1874. After this date, most of the games were produced by A N Myers; however, the dissected puzzles were issued by George Philip & Son. Unfortunately, few of Betts's works were actually dated, and many were re-issued several times. Dating is usually done by assessing the subject matter and the methods of printing and colouring.

148

5 times 7
'We're going such

are 35.
a pleasant drive.

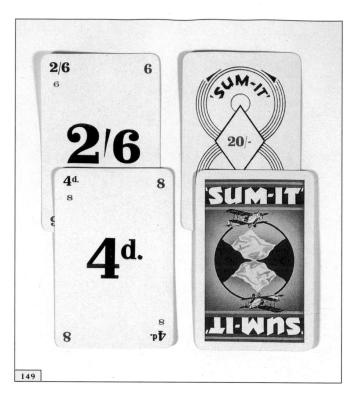

149

148

Arithmetic and music could also be taught in much the same manner. It is difficult not to wonder, however, if children really found these games as exciting, amusing or fun as their publishers claimed. Nevertheless most, but not all, are very pictorial and perhaps parents preferred to buy these card games than ones that were non-educational. *The Multiplication Table in Rhyme*, a set of hand-coloured lithographs, was published in about 1850 by John Betts. Each of the 96 cards bears half an illustration and half a caption.

149

Sum-It, which was printed by chromolithography, was published by Sum-It Card Games Ltd during the 1930s. The game is designed to teach calculation using the complex British monetary system of pounds, shillings and pence, which was replaced in the early 70s by the current decimal system. It is played by the same rules as *Happy Families*.

150

McDowalls' Musical Game was printed by letterpress. All the questions are on cards, of which there are 150 in all, while all the answers are given in a booklet. It was published in 1836 by Smith, Elder and Company.

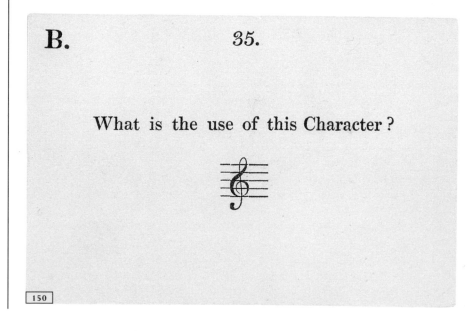

B.   **35.**

What is the use of this Character?

150

151

151

Learning the ideals of good behaviour came to be regarded as important as the 'three Rs'. The precepts were often found as proverbs on card, and again, the idea of the game is that a group has to be collected. They are often quite humorous, although it is difficult to tell if this was deliberate or merely a late 20th century interpretation of the sayings and drawings. Generally, the gambling element of rewards and forfeits were removed from the rules of these 'moral' games. *Extremes Meet*, hand-coloured etchings, has been taken from a pack of 63 cards which was published in about 1860 as *The New Game of Illustrated Proverbs*.

152

Produced as a set of woodcuts, the card game *The Royal Game of Mother Goose* uses illustrations and rhyming couplets. It was published in about 1860 by Richard Marsh.

152

153

Love Me, Love My Dog is part of a set of hand-coloured engravings. There are 64 cards in all, which must be collected to form groups, each of which contains a sentence.

THE COUNTIES OF ENGLAND

The set of rules for playing *The Counties of England* were the most popular and widely followed before the introduction of *Happy Families*. They are quite simple, and young children can play the games with ease. Like *Happy Families* and *Snap*, this game was published by John Jaques & Son of London. There are three packs, which could be sold separately or as a complete set, each of which has 61 cards, 13 cards bear the names of counties and principal towns while the rest carry pictures of those towns. One pack covers the Midland counties, the second Northern and Western counties and the third Southern and Eastern counties. The complete set of three packs was issued in a wooden box with a sliding lid.

One player has to be president, and he or she retains the 13 county cards while the rest are dealt. Each player is given six counters, of which an agreed number is put into the pool. The president asks each player in turn for a card of the town belonging to the county he names. If a card of another county is offered, the player forfeits one counter to the pool; if the right card is offered, the player takes a counter from the pool. Any player able to relate a fact or describe the scenery, products or so on connected with the card, receives an additional counter. When the sets are made up, the player with the most counters wins. The cards may, of course, also be used to play by the *Happy Families* rules.

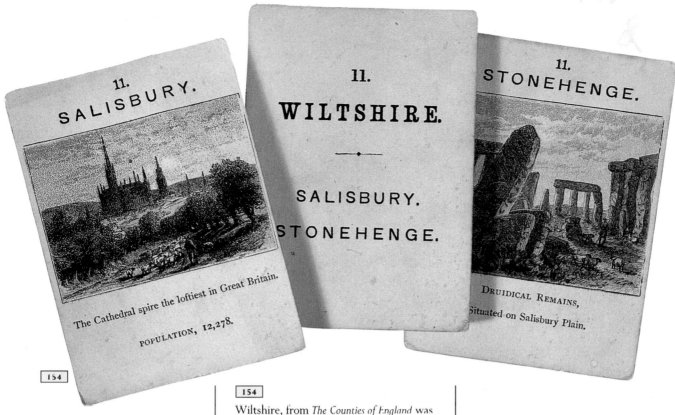

11.
SALISBURY.

The Cathedral spire the loftiest in Great Britain.

POPULATION, 12,278.

154

11.
WILTSHIRE.

—•—

SALISBURY.

STONEHENGE.

11.
STONEHENGE.

DRUIDICAL REMAINS,
Situated on Salisbury Plain.

154

Wiltshire, from *The Counties of England* was produced as hand-coloured engravings and printed by letterpress. The game was published by John Jaques & Son Ltd in about 1870. This set shows the smallest group of one county and two principal cards; other sets contain more, but there is no standard number for each county.

HAPPY FAMILIES

Perhaps the first card games devised to amuse rather than educate children were developed by John Jaques & Son of London during the 1860s. These were the games of *Happy Families* and *Snap*. The company was responsible for introducing the idea of cards showing families of four, each of which has an appropriate name relating to the father's occupation, such as Bun the Baker or Soot the Sweep. Since it was devised, *Happy Families* has been consistently popular, and many other publishers have introduced their own variations.

The rules are simple but competitive. All the cards are dealt, and the player to the left of the dealer starts by asking any of the other players for a character he or she is short of to complete a set. The player should endeavour to collect all the cards relating to one family, and when the four cards are held, they are placed, face downwards, as a trick, on the table. (The word 'trick' is really a misnomer in this game, as the aim is to collect a sequence and not to trump other cards.) If the player asked has not got the character, he or she replies 'Not at home' and it becomes his or her turn to ask. The game proceeds until all the family sets are complete, and the player holding the greatest number of tricks wins. Players cannot ask for characters unless they already hold a member of the family, and players are bound to produce the character asked for if they have it.

The game can end here or continue with following other rules. Only players holding tricks continue, and the one with the greatest number starts. He or she asks any other player for a family. If the player asked does not have the family, it then becomes his or her turn. The game ends when one player holds all the families.

An element of gambling can be introduced if each player puts an agreed number of counters into a pool. The winner of the first part of the game takes half the kitty, and the winner of the second part takes the rest.

An interesting extra to the rules of play that is incorporated into some of these card games is the paying of a special forfeit. Instead of just losing a turn, a player must allow an unseen card to be drawn from his hand by an opponent.

Although not devised for educational purposes, the *Happy Families* rules did apply, like those of *The Counties of England,* to many earlier card games. Jaques may well have simply used existing formats or, rather, standardized them for his two famous games.

155

Mr. Block the Barber.

Mr. Block the Barber.

Mrs. Block the Barber's Wife.

Mrs. Block the Barber's Wife

Master Block the Barber's Son.

Master Block the Barber'

Miss Block the Barber's Daughter.

Miss Block the Barber's Daughter.

155

Mr Block the Barber, produced as a hand-coloured lithograph, is one of the characters from the original 44-card set, designed by Sir John Tenniel, the illustrator of Lewis Carroll's *Alice's Adventures in Wonderland* and *Through the Looking Glass.* The subtitle is 'A New and Diverting Game for Juveniles' and the characters are described as 'grotesque'. Mr Block is a fine caricature of a barber with his comb and shaving brush and his carefully folded hair and tightly curled beard.

Following Jaques' first sets of *Happy Families*, many publishers copied his original idea, sometimes changing the title to *Funny Families, Cheery Families* or *Merry*

Families. During the first years of the 20th century, Thomas De La Rue & Co Ltd published a number of variations, often based on characters from well-known books. *The New and Diverting Game of Alice in Wonderland* includes scenes drawn as facsimiles by Miss E Gertrude Thomson, but original designs by Florence and Bertha Upton were used by De La Rue to illustrate *The Pictorial Game of Golliwog.*

156

Mr Baker and Family is part of a set of 24 cards printed by lithography and published by the Multum in Parvo Company of Clerkenwell Green, London in about 1900 under the title *Merry Families.* The company made many indoor games, and the illustrations used for this game are rather surrealistic; for example, each member of the Baker family is made from various bakery products.

156

SNAP

John Jaques introduced the game of *Snap* in 1866, using illustrations of 'grotesque characters' as he had for *Happy Families*. Like *Happy Families* too, *Snap* cards are arranged in groups, but each card in a group bears the same picture. The games are generally played with forfeits, and the rules are simple enough for young children to enjoy playing. The cards are dealt equally among the players, face down, and the dealer starts by turning over his or her top card to reveal an illustration. The next player to the left does likewise and, if that card matches the first, he or she 'snaps' the first player, who pays a forfeit. Should the third player also have a similar card, he or she 'snaps' the second player, who then has to pay a double forfeit. The game continues until all the players but one have lost their forfeits and that remaining player is declared the winner. The game may, of course, be played without forfeits.

157

Snap, The Old Original Game Consisting of 64 Cards of Grotesque Characters was printed by chromolithography. This is a 1930s reprint of Jaques' original cards.

SPELLING GAMES ON CARDS

All card games which aim to promote spelling skills are basically the same – a selection of letters are used to make up words. The playing rules are generally simple, with players having a choice of one of four moves. Each player is dealt 10 cards, and the remaining cards placed in a pile face down but with the top card exposed. The players take it in turn to try to form a complete word from the cards in their hands. The word is placed face up on the table, and the players discard one of their cards and take either the exposed card or a blind one. Players can add to words already formed – for example, changing 'mother' to 'smother' – or substitute letters – for example removing the e from 'expert' to form 'export'. As the game proceeds a crossword is formed, so after the fourth person's turn the table looks somewhat like a *Scrabble* board. Although the general purpose of the game is to aid spelling skills, the aim is to get rid of the cards as soon as possible.

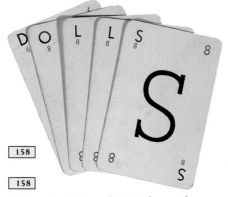

158

158

During the 1920s and 1930s these rather sophisticated card games were developed to their full potential. The best known is John Waddington's *Lexicon*, which was presented with the cards housed in a book-shaped case.

159

159

Another spelling card game, with unusual title, is *My Word, The Better Letter Game*. It was published by W & A Storey & Co Ltd of Croydon in about 1930.

160

160

Kan-U-Go, The Crossword Card Game was copyrighted in 1934 by Porterprint Ltd of Leeds. It is another good example of the spelling card game.

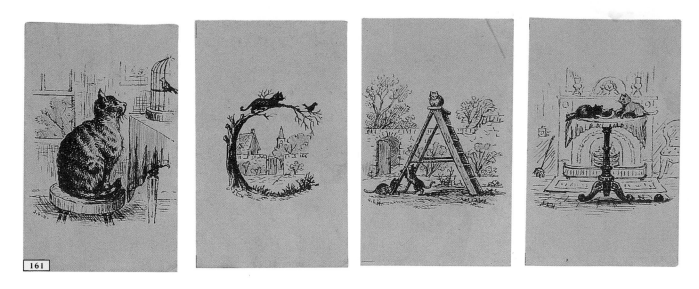

161

What was possibly the most attractive of the spelling card games was published in 1878. It is called *The New Game of Animals* and the rules state that it 'is played similarly to *Happy Families* and that the object of the players is to obtain as many complete sets as possible but several new rules are introduced affording much additional interest.' The additions to the general rules are that the design of each letter shows to which animal it belongs, but some of the letters are intentionally made rather obscure, and if players misunderstand a card, ask for one belonging to a set of which they have none or ask for a card they already hold, they lose a turn. Moreover, if players find that no one has the card for which they have asked or all their cards have already gone, they may draw a card from the pool and continue to play. The cat, drawn by J Lacy Hulbert, was published as part of *The New Game of Animals*.

HOME-MADE CARD GAMES

While the majority of card games were mass produced by known publishers, a few were made by inventive individuals. Most were designed by parents for children, but it is possible that some children produced their own. Two very attractive hand-drawn sets were made in Austria between 1900 and 1925. One is a set of questions and answers and the other a game of *Snap*.

162

A set of *Question and Answer Cards*, which are hand-drawn and painted in watercolour, was made in Austria between 1900 and 1925.

163

163

A set of *Snap* cards, also made in Austria in the first quarter of this century, are hand-drawn and painted in watercolour.

164

164

Two rather intriguing games, both products of the 1930s, are based on the principles of Crime and Punishment, a 20th century version of the good behaviour games of the 19th century. One assumes that they were designed to lead children away from crime, although they may have been intended to teach the players how to avoid detection. Shown are some of the cards from a complete set of 51 cards which formed the game *Alibi*, produced in the 1930s.

165

The second game, *Krimo, The New Game of Logical Detection*, was played with a set of 60 cards and was introduced during the 1930s.

166

Popeye the Sailor Man made his debut in the United States in 1929 and, like other cartoon characters such as Mickey Mouse, has featured in comics, strip cartoons and film cartoons. Also like Mickey Mouse the character became a games character as seen in the *Pop-Eye Playing Card Game,* published in the United States by Whitman Publishing Company and copyrighted in 1934 by the King Features Syndicate. Whitman Publishing Company of Racine, Wisconsin, is a publisher, possibly best known for its children's books.

167

Poetical Pot pie or Aunt Hilda's Courtship is an educational card game published by Milton Bradley in 1868. There are approximately 120 card strips each printed with a quote by a famous author. The instructions booklet has a story with blanks, each to be filled in by a suitable quote. The potential of the game, though strictly educational, could prove to be a great amusement as often unsuitable quotes would be used. There were many games of *Authors* published in the United Sates by all the main publishers, though by no means were the people represented all Americans or in fact living.

165

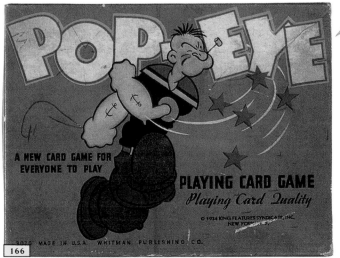

166

167

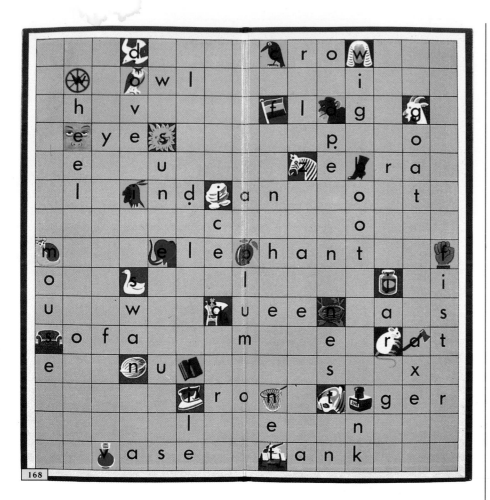

Scrabble For Juniors was published in 1983 by J W Spear & Sons plc. This board has two sides and the reverse can be used for a normal game of *Scrabble*. The picture side, however, has been designed for younger children and shows words and illustrations, which have to be covered. The players need not know how to form words from the letters they select, but they can place any letter on an appropriate square. The players gain points when they complete a word.

169

169

These letters of the alphabet are painted bone discs, which are housed in a round box. Made in about 1800, the letters can be used to create words, but they were generally used by young children to learn the letters of the alphabet. Such alphabets, made of bone and card, were used to teach children for many generations.

170

Shake-Spell consists of wooden dice with a letter of the alphabet on each of the six sides together with a cardboard dice shaker. The aim of the game is to create a word from the letters shown on the face which is shown after each throw of the dice. The winner of each turn would be the player who made not only the longest word, but also the word using the most difficult letters.

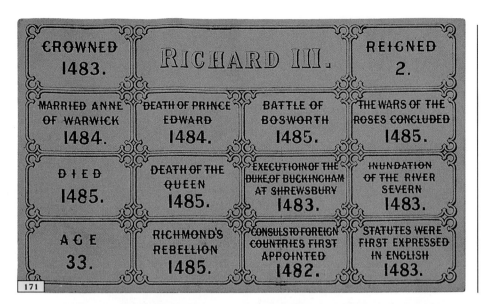

171

Lotto, which is another name for *Bingo*, has always been primarily a game of chance. Nevertheless, publishers of children's games decided to use this format as an educational tool, and John Jaques & Son, soon turned its attention to this form of play. The company, of course, was not alone and many publishers produced games of varying difficulty. Richard III is one of 35 large cards showing the English monarchs from William I to William IV in the set of *Historical Lotto*, published by John Jaques & Son Ltd of London in about 1870. The players must fill up their cards with the correct smaller cards, which are drawn from a fabric bag.

172

This is one of 12 cards showing pictures of flowers from the game *Floral Lotto, a New Round Game*. With the game are 120 oval cards, printed with the popular and botanical names of the flowers and their emblematic significance. The cards were published by John Jaques in about 1872.

173

174

173

Loto Enfantin Jeu Amusant was played in sets of six cards, of which one is shown. It was published in Paris between 1900 and 1910, and the illustrations and 72 small illustrated cards are captioned in four languages.

174

Lotto could also be used to answer general knowledge questions, similar to those posed by the modern game of *Trivial Pursuit*. Chad Valley based its game *Answerit* on *Lotto*. A number of plain large cards have to be filled in when the questions on the smaller cards have been answered correctly. The game was published in about 1925 and the cover illustration shows adults in evening dress rather than children playing this game.

GAMES, CARDS AND ADVERTISING

How often do games appear on the back of a cereal packet or on the base of a box of chocolates, especially at Christmas? Games used as promotional tools were a logical inclusion in the advertising arsenal of larger companies in about 1900 and they are still used by many companies to promote all sorts of products.

175

While some games, such as race games, actually appear on the packaging itself, others may be included as free gifts in the package or be 'send away for' items. Most of the advertising is food related, usually on items prepared for human consumption, and it is aimed at the person who will buy the products rather than the consumer, although, of course, they may be the same person. *Kings and Queens of England* was published by the Mazawattee Tea Company in Britain in about 1910. The cards cover the individual monarchs from William I to Edward VII.

176

In 1920 Milton Bradley issued the *Game of the Lost Heir,* based directly on the real life story of a kidnapped boy. The Canada Games Company simply copied the idea giving it a Canadian twist. Copying, adapting and pirating of games were common practices between companies and countries. Most methods of playing can be found in much earlier civilizations with only the presentation changed to suit the country or what the manufacturer wants to achieve. This is best seen in the race games which can be traced back to Ancient Egypt.

177

THE DISSECTED PUZZLE –
THE EARLY JIGSAW

The jigsaw puzzle has been one of the most consistently popular toys for two hundred years and has been played with by both children and adults, by individuals or groups. Completing a jigsaw puzzle requires concentration and agile fingers while remaining an essentially quiet occupation. Jigsaw puzzles are therefore considered suitable for convalescents. The jigsaw puzzles that we know today were not created until the introduction in the 1870s of the jigsaw itself, a machine with which an irregular pattern could be cut. However complicated these patterns may appear to be, modern puzzles have one saving grace – the pieces interlock and thus stay together. This was not always the case – in the past there have been puzzles and methods of cutting them that test not only the ingenuity but also the patience of many adults.

The forerunner of the jigsaw puzzle is referred to as the 'dissected puzzle' because of the method used to create it. The illustrations were simply hand-cut into shapes and few, if any, of the pieces interlocked.

A Londoner named John Spilsbury, who was born in 1739, is credited with being the first person to provide a dissected puzzle as a toy for a child. Spilsbury was apprenticed to Thomas Jefferys of St Martins Lane, London, in 1753, and in 1763 he was listed as an 'engraver and map dissector in wood, in order to facilitate the teaching of geography.'

Spilsbury took a map of the British counties, mounted it on thin mahogany board and cut by hand around each of the county boundaries. The map was then boxed and sold for a child to reassemble. He produced about 30 different map puzzles, along with a great variety of wares including books, prints, maps, charts and printed silk handkerchiefs.

John Spilsbury died in 1769, and although part of his business continued, the production of dissected maps came to an end as there was little or no interest in them. Some years later, other publishers began to produce dissected maps and they added other topics, including historical subjects, to their lines of dissected puzzles.

177

The *Bride and Groom*, published during the 1920s (see page 117).

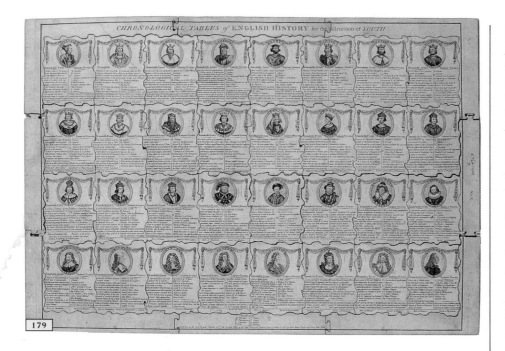

179

179

John Wallis, who was already well established as a publisher of games, also produced puzzles, which were reissued and updated when necessary. One of his earliest was entitled *Chronological Tables of English History for the Instruction of Youth*, which was published in 1788. It shows, together with brief notes about their reigns, the English monarchs from William I to George III. It was a hand-coloured engraving cut into 40 pieces. Along the bottom edge is the legend: 'Published as the Act directs March 25th, 1788 by John Wallis at his Map Warehouse, Ludgate Street, London, and sold by John Binns, Leeds, and Louis Ball, Bath.' As is common with many dissected puzzles, the outer edges have been cut to interlock, although it is necessary to place the cut-away hole over the tongue piece, as the cut itself is at an angle. The rest of the pieces simply abut, each having been cut with wavy, rather than straight, lines. As with the modern puzzle, many shapes are very similar to each other, so as a child places the pieces, he will learn that they must be put in the right way to fit together.

180

While many puzzle maps of Britain and Europe were published, those featuring the world were rarer. On September 1st, 1820 William Darton published *The World Dissected Upon The Best Principles to Teach Youth Geography*, a puzzle showing the world in two round shapes containing the eastern and western hemispheres. Apart from making some adjustments to the western edge of North America and changing the names and borders of countries and states in Europe and Africa, this map puzzle could be used today. The puzzle was a hand-coloured engraving, cut into 30 pieces.

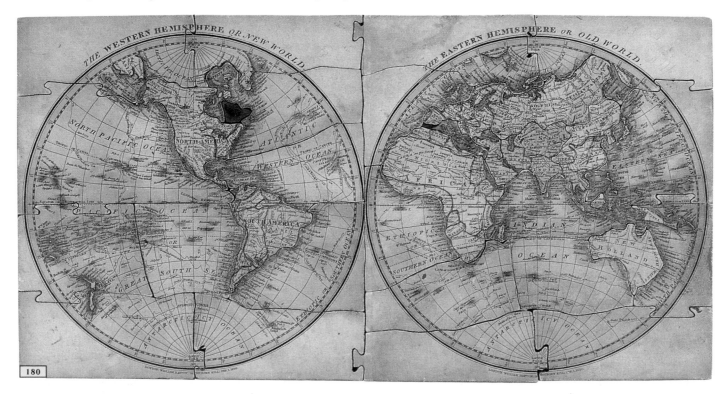

180

181

Like other types of games, dissected puzzles were used for other themes of an educational nature. *My Mother*, which was also published by William Darton, of London, in 1815, has six illustrations, each of which is supported by a text. The child would be encouraged to read the poems as the puzzle was constructed, thus assisting with both reading and dexterity skills. The puzzle is a hand-coloured engraving, cut into 33 pieces. It is subtitled 'Written expressly for that interesting little work entitled *Original Poems for Infants' Minds.*' All the figures have been cut.

WILLIAM DARTON, LONDON

Established by William Darton in 1787 at 55 Gracechurch Street, this company had a number of different partners and names. For the first four years, it was W Darton & Co, followed by Darton & Harvey when Joseph Harvey became a partner in 1791. Twenty years later, it became Darton, Harvey & Darton when Samuel Darton joined, then reverted to Harvey & Darton when William died in 1819. Depending on who was the senior partner, the name switched between Darton & Harvey and Harvey & Darton – the former in 1834 with Samuel

Darton and Robert Harvey, and the latter in 1838 with Robert Harvey and Thomas Darton. In 1847 the firm was sold to R Y Clarke.

William Darton's son, also named William, opened his own establishment in 1804 in Holborn Hill, first numbered 40 then 58. This address remained until the firm was sold in 1867 to W Wells Gardner. Like his father, William Jnr had a number of different company names. He started with 'W Darton Jun', which was in use until 1830. However, during this period 'W & T Darton' was used when Thomas

Darton was a partner between 1806 and 1811, and after 1819 'William Darton' was often used. 'William Darton & Son' was in use from 1830 to 1836 when John Maw Darton became a partner. He joined with Samuel Clark for 10 years to become Darton & Clark, and from 1846 to 1862 worked alone as Darton & Co. John Maw Darton again used this imprint shortly before his firm was sold, but between 1862 and 1866, 'Darton & Hodge' may be found, with an address of 175 The Strand, when he was joined by Robert Hodge.

Interesting events were also portrayed, as were the new trades and industries, and changing design styles to shape a particular pattern were introduced. Processions, for example, were shown in tiers, usually three or four, to give the impression of a long line. *The Lord Mayor's Show* was published as a hand-coloured engraving. Still a sight to behold on a cold November day in London, the show no longer has the water barges as part of the main procession, although many can be seen in celebration on the River Thames.

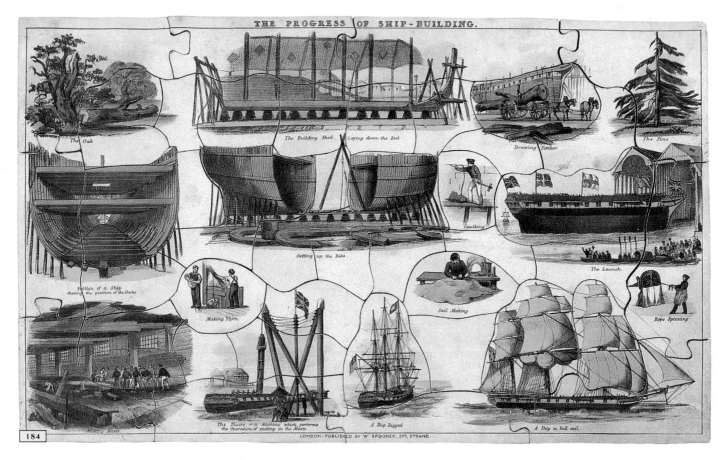

184

LONDON: PUBLISHED BY W. SPOONER, 377, STRAND.

184

Another mid-19th century dissected puzzle showing the importance of industry is William Spooner's *The Progress of Ship Building*, a hand-coloured lithograph cut into 42 pieces. The puzzle reveals the importance attached to national industries and most of the scenes have been carefully cut around to keep them intact.

183

London, Birmingham, Liverpool and Manchester Railway was published as a hand-coloured engraving, cut into 69 pieces, by William Peacock in about 1860. The illustration shows a very long train on the two centre tiers and buildings connected with the cities on the outer tiers. The railway puzzle uses an illustration, dating from about 1840, which is probably the work of Edward Wallis, but it is much more significant as it has another puzzle on the reverse side – a map of England and Wales. Such puzzles are called double dissection and the full title of this particular example is *Peacock's Improved Double Dissection, England and Wales*.

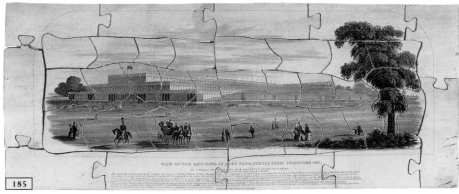

185

185

The Great Exhibition which was held in London in 1851, inspired many games and puzzles. The building itself, made of glass and cast iron, brought visitors from far and wide to view its structure. It contained international displays that would be the pride of many a modern exhibition. *View of the Building in Hyde Park for the Great Exhibition*, 1851 is a hand-coloured aquatint cut into 40 pieces. This particular puzzle was published by C. Berger.

186

187

186

Joy Ride is a 119-piece wooden jigsaw puzzle issued in the 1930s under the series title Paramount Jig-Saw Puzzle. It was produced by the Salem Puzzle Company of Bridge Street, Salem, Massachusetts, which was a subsidiary of Parker Brothers. Parker Brothers issued several lines of jigsaw puzzles and was the leading American producer during the first half of the 20th century. One line was the Pastime Picture Puzzle noted for its intricate figural and geometric shapes. Other lines which were less expensive were marketed under the names Climax, Jig-a-Jag and Jig Wood. The Paramount Jig-Saw Puzzles lacked figural pieces, were largely non-interlocking and may have been cut by apprentices.

187

Many 20th century jigsaw puzzles were cut to suit the age and ability of children, and they show a progression from large, easily managed pieces with simple, recognizable pictures to smaller pieces with complex or even abstract images. Two such puzzles, both contained within a surround for easy control, show 'role playing' themes. Unfortunately neither bears any clues to their publishers. *Mothers and Fathers* was printed by chromolithography and it is pasted on plywood which has been cut into 24 pieces. The puzzle is contained within a wooden and hardboard tray. This puzzle was played with by children attending a primary school from the 1950s to the 1980s.

NO DOGS ALLOWED

Here is a little picture as a guide to the jig-saw on the opposite page. You can paint this picture.

They put a new roof on
Doggie-Town School
And while they were busy
the dogs had to go—
Jim the Alsatian
And Dick the Dalmatian
And fat little snuffily
Willie the Bull—
To the class that is kept
in Pussy-Cat Row
By funny old Dame Kitty
Whiskers, you know.

The doggies had hopes
of oceans of fun
In teasing the poor little
pussy-cats there
By horrible scowling
And terrible growling.
You wouldn't believe the
things that were done.
The poor pussies cried,
and wept in despair
The teasing was greater
than pussies could bear.

But Dame Kitty Whiskers
she sprang a surprise.
There wasn't a dog that
could frighten Dame K.
She out with her cane and
They shouted with pain
and,
Ere you could count two,
with tears in their eyes
They were out at the door,
and had bolted away.
They *were* model pupils
the following day.

188

NO DOGS ALLOWED

188

No Dogs Allowed was also printed by chromolithography but it is pasted on cardboard which has been cut into 54 interlocking pieces. This puzzle is one of five contained in a child's book, entitled *The Jolly Jig-Saw Book*. Each puzzle has a story, written as a poem, to be read aloud by a child or by an adult, and the guide picture at the top may be coloured in too. Such a publication seems to have been designed to test many abilities, and was printed in about 1935.

189

189

Rather more frivolous, and probably designed for adults or older children, is a shaped jigsaw that has been cut without the conventional straight border, making the puzzle more life-like. The shape emerges as the puzzle is completed, and none of the pieces interlocks. It is quite unstable and the pieces dislodge easily. Nevertheless, it is an intriguing puzzle of an amusing subject. The *Bride and Groom* puzzle is a chromolithograph illustration that has been cut into 175 pieces. It was published during the 1920s under the name *The Figure-It-Out English Jigsaw Puzzle*. The picture gives the impression that the couple are dancing, but they are in fact departing and being showered with confetti.

117

189

Auctioneer, The Antique Dealers' Game,
published by Uniray (UK) Ltd in 1959 (see
page 122).

AMERICAN GAMES

At first, children's games and other board games were imported into America from Britain and the rest of Europe. Before too long, however, Americans were producing their own games and manufacturers like George S Parker began to dominate the international scene. When American production began, it was primarily centred in the New England towns around Boston and in New York. One of the most famous was W & S B Ives of Salem, Massachusetts, who published *The Mansion of Happiness.*

190

The Mansion of Happiness, an Instructive, Moral and Entertaining Amusement is claimed to be the first board game actually published in the United States. Published by W & S B Ives of Salem, Massachusetts in 1843, it bears great similarities to the 1800 Laurie and Whittle game of the same name (see page 53). The American edition is said to have been the idea of a Miss Anne W Abbott, the daughter of a New England minister, but it is more likely that, if she actually had anything to do with the game, she might have presented it to the publishers as a game that might 'properly' be played by children.

The British and American versions are slightly different – the Laurie and Whittle one is more angular in design, for example – but the illustrated compartments and even the central picture are almost identical. The game was reissued several times, and by other publishers, including Parker Brothers in 1894.

190

W & S B IVES, SALEM, MASSACHUSETTS

W & S B Ives began in 1830 and their products were eventually absorbed by George S Parker in 1887. They are listed as the first American publishers and produced board games and card games, *including* Trades, Yankee Trader *and* Uncle Tom's Cabin. *The name Ives crops up in various New England towns in relation to games and toys in general. Possibly* the best known company under this name is that of E R Ives of Plymouth which started as Ives, Blakeslee & Co, makers and patentees of many toys and dolls, particularly mechanical ones.

191

W & S B Ives, a company that is later recorded as S B Ives, was established in 1830 in Salem, a town just a few miles outside Boston, where to this day the prominent publishers and games makers, Parker Brothers, are still located. The Ives company produced both card and board games, illustrating many styles and often with very original titles. In 1844 it produced a Fox and Geese board entitled *The Game of Pope and Pagan* or *Siege of the*

Stronghold of Satan by the Christian Army, followed two years later by *Mahomet and Saladin* or *The Battle for Palestine* another Fox and Geese board.

The company also produced card games, the first *Dr Busby* appeared in 1843 and was followed by *Menagerie, Trades, Yankee Trader, Uncle Tom's Cabin, Heroes* and *Master Redbury and His Pupils*. This example is taken from *The Game of Trades*, which is a card game with a set of 48 hand-coloured lithographed cards.

Published by W & S B Ives, the set includes eight illustrated cards (pictured here) and 40 cards showing only the trade symbols. The aim of the game is to collect the card of each trade, and so to make a trick. Basically the rules of *Happy Families* apply, and it may well be that while the *Mansion of Happiness* is an American version of a British game, *Happy Families* may conversely be a British adaption of an American game. *The Game of Trades* was reissued by Parker Brothers in 1889.

MILTON BRADLEY, SPRINGFIELD, MASSACHUSETTS

Established about 1860, the company is still active as a prolific games producer. While publishing games, in 1867 the firm issued the Zoetrope, a 'moving picture' toy consisting of a drum shape with slits in the sides and which was mounted on a stand. A strip of images each with a slightly modified pose was placed inside the drum and when it was spun and the images viewed through the slits, movement appeared to occur. In 1920, Milton Bradley bought out McLoughlin Brothers, another large and successful publisher of games.

192

193

192

The Popular Game of Innocence Abroad, which is a chromolithograph, combines two difficult games. The first part involves a shopping expedition, which is represented (at the top left corner) by a grid of 48 squares, some of which have instructions for movements and forfeits. Having passed through the grid, the players begin the second part of the game. They depart for the city by means of a straightforward route that runs through a variety of scenic areas and detours, involving several possible methods of travel. The first player to reach the city may not be the eventual winner, as the winner is determined by the overall cost of the trip. Although this is an enjoyable game to play, players are constantly made aware of the dangers of wasting both time and money.

This version of *The Popular Game of Innocence Abroad* was published by Parker Brothers about 1918, the year the company presented the copy to the Essex Institute of Salem, Massachusetts. It was copyrighted in 1888 and 'Entered according to the Act of Congress in the year 1888 by Geo. S Parker & Co. in the Office of the Librarian of Congress at Washington, DC.' This rubric marks a change, as many of the games were entered at the offices of the District Court of Massachusetts. The game was produced from 1888 to 1931 and little changed throughout that time.

193

In another Massachusetts' town, Springfield, an enterprising young man acquired a lithography press and quickly began to issue the games that became the foundation for another great American toy company, Milton Bradley. The first game, *The Checkered Game of Life* was issued in 1860 and it is very similar to early versions of *Snakes and Ladders* and *Kismet*, although it uses hands to indicate the direction of moves.

The Checkered Game of Life was printed by chromolithography and entered by Milton Bradley with the copyright date 1863. It is marked on the cover as being 'Published by D B Brooks & Bros, Salem'. A second issue of the game, which went on to be published many times, was patented by Milton Bradley on March 30th, 1866.

194

194

The Game of Going to Sunday School is a moral game which used a teetotum rather than a spinner or dice. It was published by McLoughlin Brothers in 1885 as a lithograph mounted on a folded board. It shows the pitfalls children, especially boys, may experience and the punishments that befall them.

195

Rather a cross between a board game and a table game was the McLoughlin Brothers *Game of Four and Twenty Blackbirds,* published in 1908. Each bird has a number or value and they are set up in the pie. A spinner is used to determine the value of the bird that the player must attempt to catch by using a fishing pole, and the player with the greatest value of blackbirds, rather than the player with the greatest number of actual birds, wins.

195

196

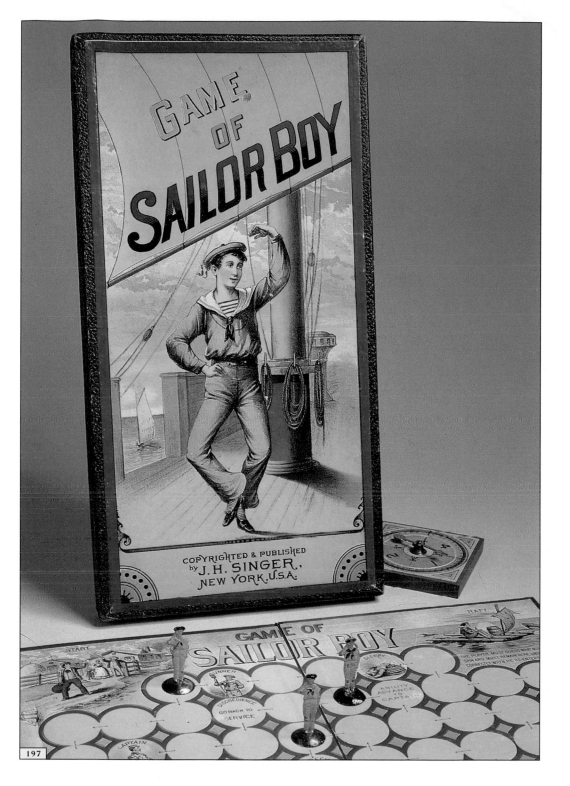

197

196

The Game of the Newsboy is a combination of a board and a card game. It was published by the R Bliss Company in 1890. The playing surface shows a fascinating lithograph giving the names of the major newspapers of American cities at the time.

197

In 1889 and 1890, two games were issued by relatively unknown games makers and both games feature the name boy in their titles. *The Game of the Sailor Boy* was copyrighted and published by J H Singer of New York City in 1889. The game is a race game with forfeits and rewards. Moves are governed by a spinner but rather than following a numbered sequence, the players follow arrows from one circle to another, sometimes forwards and at other times backwards.

GAMES OF MONEY

It is perhaps only in the United States that games could be developed around making money, playing the Stock Exchange and buying and selling property. In many of the games issued by American publishers during the 19th century it is possible to detect the important part played by the idea of becoming 'a success', and this theme was developed and grew during the early years of the 20th century. Although the most famous game that has survived is *Monopoly*, it was just one of many, and its own history is very checkered.

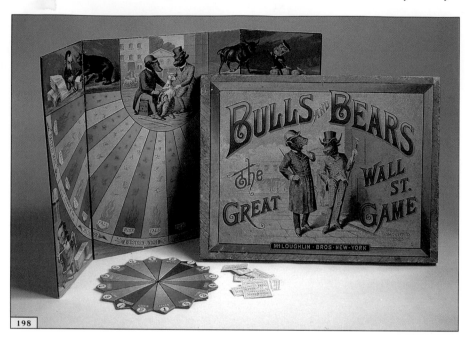

198

199

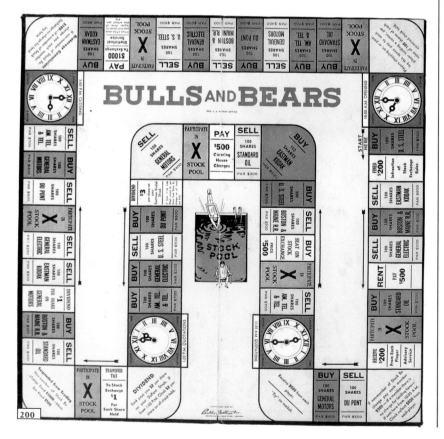

198

The workings of the Stock Exchange form the basis of several games, published by various companies including McLoughlin Brothers and Parker Brothers. In 1883, McLoughlin Brothers patented *Bulls and Bears The Great Wall Street Game.* It is a fine example of a chromolithograph mounted on a three-way folded board and uses a spinner to determine the play.

199

In 1904 a card game was issued by Parker Brothers and titled *Pit.* The players' aim was to collect a complete set of nine cards of one commodity and thus 'corner the market'. Later the idea of bull and bear markets (rising and falling prices) was introduced into the game, where they affected the counting of points awarded to and against the players.

200

The board game *Bulls and Bears* was copyrighted by Parker Brothers in 1936 and its cover illustration bears a picture and the signature of Charles B Darrow, who was long thought to have been the inventor of Monopoly. This game reflects the trading day of the Stock Market, from its opening at 10am to the close at 3pm.

201

Monopoly, on the other hand, has proved to be a great success, and it is still in production in a variety of editions reflecting various countries. Parker Brothers bought the rights to the game from Charles B Darrow, who claimed to have invented the game. However, similar games had been played by many, often using home made boards. The first game to use the idea of land rents, taxes and monopolies was *The Landlord's Game* which was devised by Elizabeth Magie Phillips and published in 1904. During the late 1920s, hand made games, painted on sheets of oilcloth, were made and sold by members of the Religious Society of Friends (Quakers) in Atlantic City. It was one of these games that Charles Darrow presented to Parker Brothers, which bought the rights and began production in 1935. Unfortunately Darrow failed to reveal the true origins of the game.

202

Published at the same time as *Monopoly* was a game which combined educational ideas with money making ideas. Copyrighted in 1936 by the Transgram Company of New York City and given the name *Big Business, The Newest National Money Game,* it may have helped the players familiarize themselves with the various states which make up the United States as well as each state's strengths and weaknesses.

INDEX

BIBLIOGRAPHY

ARNOLD, ARNOLD
The World of Children's Games
MacMillan London Ltd, London, 1975.

BELL, R C
Winners
Paladin Grafton Books, London, 1989.

Board and Table Games from many Civilizations
O U P, London, 1960.

Discovering Old Board Games
Shire Publications, Aylesbury, 1976.

Games to Play
Michael Joseph Ltd, London, 1988.

The Boardgame Book
The Knapp Press, Los Angeles, 1979.

BETT, HENRY
The Games of Children: Their Origins & History
Methuen & Co. Ltd, London, 1929.

CASSELL & CO
Cassell's Book of Indoor Amusements, Card Games and Fireside Fun, 1881.
Cassell & Co, London, 1973.

COOPER, ROSALEEN
Games from an Edwardian Childhood
David & Charles, London, 1982.

DAIKEN, LESLEY
Children's Games throughout the Year
B T Batsford Ltd, London, 1949.

DIAGRAM GROUP, THE
Waddingtons Illustrated Encyclopaedia of Games
Pan Books Ltd, London, 1984.

The Way to Play
Paddington Press, London, 1975.

GIRARD, A R & QUETEL, C
L'Histoire de France Racontee par Le Jeu de L'Oie
Ballard/Massin, France, 1982.

GOMME, ALICE B
The Traditional Games of England, Scotland and Ireland
Thames & Hudson, London, 1984.

GOULD, D W
The Top: Universal Toy, Enduring Pastime
Bailey Bros. & Swinfen Ltd, Folkestone, 1975.

GRUNFELD, FREDERIC V
Games of the World
Holt Rinehart & Winston, New York, 1975.

HANNAS, LINDA
The English Jigsaw Puzzle: 1760–1890
Wayland Publishers, London, 1972.

The Jigsaw Book
Hutchinson, London, 1981.

HOLE, CHRISTINA
English Sports and Pastimes
Batsford Ltd, London, 1949.

ICKIS, MARGUERITE
The Book of Games and Entertainment the World Over
Dodd & Mead, New York, 1969.

JEWELL, BRIAN
Sports and Games: History and Origins
Midas Books, Tunbridge Wells, 1977.

JOHARI, HARISH
Leela, Game of Knowledge
Routledge & Kegan Paul Ltd, London, 1980.

JOYNSON, D C
A Guide for Games
Kaye & Ward, London, 1969.

KEMPSON, EWART
Your Book of Card Games
Faber & Faber Ltd, London, 1966.

LOVE, BRIAN
Great Board Games
Bookclub Associates, London, 1979.

Play the Game
Michael Joseph, London, 1978.

MACCUAIG, D & CLARK, G S
Games Worth Playing
Longmans, Green & Co, London, 1940.

MCKECHNIE, SAMUEL
Popular Entertainments through the Ages
Sampson Low, Marston & Co Ltd, London, 1931.

MANN, SYLVIA
Collecting Playing Cards
Bell Publishing Co, New York, 1966.

NEWELL, WILLIAM W
Games and Songs of American Children
Dover Publications, New York, 1963.

OPIE, IONA AND PETER
Children's Games in Street and Playground
O U P, Oxford, 1979.

PENNYCOOK, ANDREW
The Indoor Games Book
Faber & Faber Ltd, London, 1973.

PICK, J B
The Phoenix Dictionary of Games
Phoenix House, London, 1965 (3rd revised edition).

PLUNTKY, PETER
Alla Tiders Spiel
Askild & Kärnekull, Stockholm, 1983.

PROVENZO, ASTERIL & EUGENE, F
Play it again: Historic Board Games you can make and play
Prentice Hall Inc., New Jersey, 1981.

REEVES, BOLEYNE
Colburn's Kalendar of Amusements for 1840
Henry Colburn, London, 1840.

RUTLEY, CECILY M
Games for Children
Thomas Nelson & Sons Ltd, London.

VINEY, NIGEL & GRANT, NEIL
An Illustrated History of Ball Games
Bookclub Associates, London, 1978.

WHITEHOUSE, F R B
Table Games of Georgian and Victorian Days
Priory Press Ltd, 1971.

WHITTON, BLAIR
Paper Toys of the World
Hobby House Press Inc., Cumberland, 1986.

CATALOGUES

ESSEX INSTITUTE
Instructive and Amusing, Essays on Toys, Games and Education in New England
Essex Institute Historical Collections, Salem, 1987.

HIMMELHEBER, GEORG
Spiele
Bayerisches Nationalmuseum, Munich, 1972.

JONES, DAVID
Toy with the Idea
Norfolk Museum Service, Norwich, 1980.

VON LEYDEN, RUDOLF
Ganjifa: The Playing Cards of India
Victoria and Albert Museum, London, 1982.

VON WILCKENS, LEONIE
Spiel, Spiele Kinderspiel
Germanisches Nationalmuseum, Nuremberg, 1985.